Leading
CONNECTED CLASSROOMS

This book is dedicated to my incredible wife Sandra, who has grown to understand my deep desire to connect to incredible people doing incredible things in incredible places around the planet. She has been an amazing partner in this journey, and has taught me so much about the power of listening, being present, and catching story. Connecting with her has allowed me to create the most vivid memories of my life.

Leading CONNECTED CLASSROOMS

ENGAGING THE HEARTS AND SOULS OF LEARNERS

ROBERT DILLON

SAGE | AdvantEDGE Teacher Resources

Los Angeles | London | New Delhi
Singapore | Washington DC | Melbourne

Originally published in 2015 by

CORWIN
A SAGE Company

Corwin
A SAGE Company
2455 Teller Road
Thousand Oaks, CA 91320
www.corwin.com

This SAGE AdvantEDGE edition published in 2017 by

SAGE | AdvantEDGE Teacher Resources

SAGE Publications India Pvt Ltd
B1/I-1 Mohan Cooperative Industrial Area
Mathura Road
New Delhi 110 044, India

Published by Vivek Mehra for SAGE Publications India Pvt Ltd and printed at Chaman Printers Pvt Ltd, New Delhi.

ISBN: 978-93-860-6235-2 (PB)

Contents

Preface

Connection: The Heart and Soul of Teaching and Learning

RATIONALE

The complexity of the teaching profession has grown tremendously. Teachers are being asked to serve a multitude of roles for kids including nurse, social worker, and life mentor. Couple this with the rigors of new standards, regulations, and requirements and the growing pressures to meet a success defined almost solely by test scores in math and reading, and it is easy to see the squeeze on our classroom teachers. Many now wonder about the sustainability of the profession without a revisioning of how teaching and learning take place.

Even with this pressure building, learning has flourished in some of our schools. As many classrooms have lost their drive to engage students with the best practices of education, some have found a way to resist the external pressures and build beautiful spaces of learning for kids. In these pockets of excellence, teachers have shown courage to continue to bring deep learning to the students they serve.

These stories of classroom success are often buried behind classroom doors and schoolhouse walls because to be public about these stories as an educator can mean being punished by supervisors for stepping out of line and not focusing on the demands of state and federal leaders and legislators. Telling these stories also means the potential scrutiny of the other teachers who have shown little courage and don't want to be exposed as mediocre. These are the teachers who are following the daily script, abandoning subjects like science, social studies, and the arts to focus on the testable subjects, and who are managing the classroom in a way that coerces students into learning. These teachers apply great pressure on schools and potential innovation as they don't want to be seen as inferior by the dedicated teacher down the hall. Many of the teachers featured for their courage in the book have experienced these pressures, and they have all persevered in difficult situations and shown a deep conviction in overcoming many obstacles.

Many of the featured teachers, leaders, and programs are often an oasis in the learning desert for the kids whom they serve. Many teachers around them aren't pushing for excellence at the rate or intensity that they are. This doesn't mean that these most innovative of teachers are without friends and allies in their buildings, but they are often without soulmates in their mission and drive for excellence.

Our connected world and the opportunity to be a connected educator has started to alleviate this pressure for some teachers. By connecting to other like-minded educators around the country, they are finding solace in the fact that there are others who are handling the same pressures. These kindred spirits, emboldened by the energy of allies and education soulmates, continue to forge ahead. They are building the teaching and learning environment that they know brings energy and excitement to student learning. The stories in this book are full of hope about meeting the needs of the whole child. They are a canvas of courage that brings new color and texture to the overwhelming volume of conversations about test scores and data, and most important, they showcase the importance of the joy in learning.

PURPOSE

This book, designed for all teachers and teacher leaders pursuing a deep learning model, focuses on connection and its power in learning. It provides energy, ideas, and a rationale for growing as a connected educator. Being connected means looking at a learning space in a very different way. It means seeing excellence in messiness because kids have an opportunity to fail forward. It means knowing the importance of flexibility so that kids have the opportunity to grow at the pace they need. The best-connected educators see excellence in asking great questions that engage kids in the purpose of their learning. They are the type of teachers that all children need and all parents want. They deeply understand that the purpose of learning is to strengthen the individual, strengthen the classroom, and strengthen the community. They see ideas as gems worth polishing and big, hairy global issues as the place to start.

In these connected classrooms, there are educators and learners dedicated not only to the classroom, but to serving education in general by collaborating with classrooms around the planet. Connected classrooms are living ecosystems that need partners and support to make their dreams possible. When visitors enter these classrooms, they feel something different, and they often struggle to put the right words to the experience. What they are feeling is empathy, and what they are seeing is thinking and conversation at their highest levels. They are also experiencing a rhythm that feels like a dance. It is the complex dance of learning displayed with elegant simplicity.

It is amazing how many teachers around the world may know about the excellence in a connected classroom before the teacher next door or the principal in the building can recognize the same. Connected teachers are sharing their best stuff freely and openly. Transparency and openness allow like-minded classroom leaders to work together for excellence.

This book was written in the hope that it will shine a bright light on the power of connection in classrooms around the country and nudge all of its readers to lean toward the opportunities of deeper learning that surround connected learning.

ORGANIZATION OF THE BOOK

There is beauty buried in classrooms throughout the country, and this book provides such a small sample of the inspiring work that is happening everywhere. There are brushfires of connection everywhere, but in too many places, the oxygen is getting sucked out of the fire. Kids, our future leaders and agents of change, deserve classrooms and schools that are inspirational and where good is never good enough.

Each chapter of the book has a group of guiding essential questions. They allow the reader an opportunity to preview the concepts and ideas that are explored in the chapter, and they serve as entry points to additional conversations around connected learning. The theory section in each chapter works through the major ideas and concepts with a focus on the big ideas. Readers also have the opportunity to explore a classroom connection written by connected educators who tell their stories of courage and connection that have deeply impacted them and the kids they serve. Each chapter concludes with a set of action steps and resources to propel the reader forward. Change and excellence ultimately come from the actions that follow the words.

Learning in the connected classroom spills into the hallways, outside of the building, and into the community. Learning like this can't be trapped. Learning like this allows us all, child and adult, to dream bigger, smile more, and achieve happiness. The hope is the reader can use these pages to grow, reflect, and be inspired by other connected educators.

Acknowledgments

Each chapter features a "Classroom Connection" from an educator who was able to bring more engagement into the classroom or school through the combination of technology tools and best practice. These stories bring the ideas of this book to life and connect best practices into daily practice. Each of these teachers and leaders is extraordinary as they bring the hope, energy, and passion to learning that all kids should experience. I thank them deeply for their contributions to the book, and I'm proud to call them friends, learning partners, and mentors. These educators are, in order of appearance:

1. J. P. Prezzavento
2. Bill Powers
3. Laura Gilchrist
4. Julie Szaj
5. Kristy Daniels-Jackson
6. Kathy Bellew
7. Christine Ruder
8. Dave Steward
9. Rob Lamb
10. Jennifer Tiller
11. William Chamberlain
12. Chris McGee
13. Kevin Grawer
14. Patrick Dempsey
15. Steve Himes
16. Steve J. Moore
17. Krissy Venosdale

PUBLISHER'S ACKNOWLEDGMENTS

Corwin gratefully acknowledges the following reviewers for their editorial insight and guidance:

Angela Becton, AIG Coordinator
Johnston County Schools
Smithfield, NC

Amanda Dykes, 6th Grade Science Teacher
McAdory Middle School
McCalla, AL

Sheila Fredericks, Technology Teacher
Mother of Providence Regional Catholic School
Wallingford, PA

Susan Herder, Instructional Technology Coordinator
Mounds View Public Schools
Shoreview, MN

Troy Hicks, Associate Professor of English
Central Michigan University
Mt. Pleasant, MI

Grant Montgomery, Principal
Moira Secondary School
Belleville, ON

Dr. Melissa Nixon, Director of Title I
Guilford County Schools
Greensboro, NC

Craig Yen, 5th Grade Teacher
Valle Verde Elementary
Walnut Creek, CA

About the Author

Dr. Robert Dillon serves the students and community of the Affton School District as director of technology and innovation. Prior to this position, he served as a teacher and administrator in public schools throughout the Saint Louis area. Dr. Dillon has a passion to change the educational landscape by building excellent engaging schools for all students. He looks for ways to ignite positive risk taking in teachers and students and release trapped wisdom into the system by growing networks of inspired educators. Dr. Dillon has had the opportunity to speak throughout the country at local, state, and national conferences as well as share his thoughts and ideas in a variety of publications. He is supported by his wife, Sandra, and two daughters, Emily and Ellie. Dr. Dillon is also an avid runner, reader, and cyclist.

CHAPTER 1

Sharing and Collaboration

The Engine for the Connected Classroom

ESSENTIAL QUESTIONS

1. How does courage emerge in a connected classroom?
2. What does it feel like to share with vigor? What emerges from adding this to your professional routine?
3. How do you break the inertia of a school culture to ignite new learning?

THE THEORY

The desire to share is human. When people ask for assistance, there is a natural urge to say yes. It may take time from the day or attention away from the focus of the moment, but to serve others brings great pleasure. In schools, there are many moments when teachers are asked to assist those who share their learning space. Teachers cover classrooms for doctor's appointments. They share kids with another class for a meeting that pops up and print sub plans when their colleagues are away. All of these speak to the natural human urge to share, support, and help.

Scaling this sharing and collaborating to truly amplify genuine instruction remains a work in progress. Even in a time when the resources and tools are plentiful to allow it to happen, teachers are not sharing and collaborating at high rates across school boundaries. Both structural and attitudinal barriers remain. Ask a prospective teacher candidate about three teachers outside the school with whom they deeply collaborate on an ongoing basis, and except for a few, rare occasions, they don't have a quality response to the question.

Why is this cross-school, cross-state, cross-country sharing essential? It is a simple case of ideas amplification. The best ideas are always as fragmented as a jigsaw puzzle. Some pieces are being used in one classroom, while other important pieces are found in another. It takes deep sharing across many classrooms to bring together the puzzle pieces that are needed to maximize learning.

All teachers want to grow as professionals, and all teachers accept that change will happen (even if they don't like it), but they need fresh models on how to share and collaborate in this connected learning ecosystem. Those that are connecting and leading connected classrooms are eagerly searching for the best ideas, resources, and materials from every place possible. Teachers in these connected spaces understand that a deep level of sharing by more and more teachers can build the network of resources needed to wrap around all places of learning. Connected classrooms also believe in the marketplace of ideas and the need for ideas and concepts to simmer over time, under the pressure and scrutiny of use, by students in multiple classrooms.

Habitual sharing also means growing more and more comfortable with criticism and questions of clarification. Teachers wanting to grow into this way of thinking and leading their classroom may need to ask if they are ready to be wrong, fail publicly, and have a perpetual stream of doubters about what they see as best practices.

THE CLASSROOM CONNECTION

J. P. Prezzavento serves as the instructional technology coordinator for a school district in Arnold, Missouri, where he helps teachers create authentic learning experiences for students. Previously, J. P. was a high school English language arts teacher who empowered his students to succeed by giving them voice and choice in their learning and used technology to give his students a global audience with whom they could share their learning.

Used with permission from J. P. Prezzavento.

A few years ago, I grew more dedicated to sharing and collaborating in a generous way. I shared because I wanted to grow as an educator, and I was eager to reach new levels for my students. One of the first things that I did to start this journey was to move all of my unit resources into a shareable space. In the beginning, I placed the resources on a classroom website as well as used a number of collaborative online resources to breathe new life into my units of study. I then started to share my units with other teachers in my school and beyond.

In addition to this move, I had been thinking of presenting at a conference for some time, but I hadn't built the courage. For me, it wasn't so much about presenting in front of adults, as I had successfully led many professional development sessions, but it was about getting past the idea that I had nothing to offer. I believe that too often teachers are overly humble about the incredible things that are happening in their classrooms, and it led me to realize that presenting ideas wasn't about being polished and perfect but about stimulating thinking, sparking new connections, and setting off a chain reaction of secondary conversations.

Every teacher has a story to tell, and that idea led me to discuss how I was sharing and growing by being more transparent with my work. Ultimately, I wanted colleagues who had big dreams for kids, and I hoped that my transparency would support their work. During this time, I met my new connected tribe at an edcamp event in town. These events build a culture that attracts innovative, energetic professionals. Since the event, I have cultivated these new professional connections.

I have also increased the sharing of the learning in my classroom. I regularly post pictures and videos, and I encourage my students to create media to share their learning journey from a student lens. This transparency has provided a learning narrative for parents and the local community, and I also hope that it will spark others around me to do the same.

ACTION STEPS

(Note: In each chapter's action steps, there will be *** by the action steps specifically designed for classroom, building, and district leaders who are new to growing a connected classroom.)

1. **Amplify your online presence with Twitter.** Using Twitter to share ideas and resources can begin to build a habit of collaboration. There are weekly chats and ongoing hashtags for every subject and specialty.
2. **Built a cohort of allies that come from within the school and beyond.** It is essential to have your ideas, resources, and materials flowing through a network.

***3. **Look for public audiences for your work and the work of your students.** Begin using the mental model that your classroom is a museum, a place for others to visit, enjoy, and learn.

RESOURCES

The links for this chapter focus on some great places for those new to the connected learning space to begin. They include online learning spaces that aggregate great content and ideas for use in the classroom. There is also information on the concept of school as a museum that can be adapted for a classroom looking to fill the classroom walls with great learning and great additional learning opportunities for kids.

Livebinders (http://www.livebinders.com/welcome/home)

Wikispaces (https://www.wikispaces.com/)

Getting Started on Twitter (http://www.livebinders.com/play/play/34291)

School as a Museum (http://bit.ly/Schoolasmuseum)

Pinterest (http://www.pinterest.com/all/education)

CHAPTER 2

Respecting the Power of Student Choice

ESSENTIAL QUESTIONS

1. How can a teacher overcome resistance from students, parents, and colleagues around providing an increasing amount of student choice?
2. What is the right balance of choice in the classroom?
3. Why would a connected educator bring additional choice into the classroom?

THE THEORY

Students deserve choice and the sense of freedom that comes from making choices, but rarely do schools live up to those needs. The bells, the master schedule, the course calendar, and the lack of opportunities to showcase learning, just to name a few of the many inhibitors of choice, tighten the noose around the educational free-will of our innately passionate learners. Classrooms are historically places that limit choices and, instead, create the conditions for students to feel trapped in the institutional education box.

Lack of student choice often comes from a lack of teacher choice. Many teachers feel trapped about what they can teach and how they can teach it. In some classrooms, teachers must follow the same pacing guide as other teachers in their building, no matter the learning opportunities available beyond the guide. These restrictions are ultimately felt by the students. When the principal is worried about curriculum coverage, and she sees her primary goal as excellent test scores, it is again the students who feel this pressure on time, resources, and opportunities. This pyramid scheme of pressure lands most heavily on the learners in the classroom.

Choice in learning is a beautiful, energizing place for those who have experienced it. It allows creativity to surface. It allows interest and iteration to naturally flourish. The need for choice seems obvious, especially when you observe children who have been without choice for years. They tense up at the opportunity to choose. Students without choice may sit for a long time hoping that the teacher gets them started with an idea, or they may just do the same thing as the person next to them. Students who haven't had the opportunity to showcase their learning based on their choice stress having options. They can even resent choice. Many teachers react to this by adding in limits and being more prescriptive. Doing this is just treating the symptoms as opposed to dealing with the problem. Classrooms that fall into the trap that students don't want or need choice based on students' initial reactions are leaving students ill prepared for their learning beyond high school.

The connected classroom leans into this challenge for greater choice by slowly reintroducing choice into the space of learning. This reintroduction works best when all teachers who surround a group of students participate, because without consistent choice in all classes, the road to comfort takes longer. Students in the early opportunities of having choice view classrooms with many choices as their hardest classes because often the students are used to looking for a checklist to an A grade instead of looking to produce excellent work. This creates tension for individuals and the classroom as a whole, and the connected educator has to make space to discuss these feelings. Through open classroom conversation, students can grow to see the true power of student choice, and this begins to peel away the stress that can mount in connected classrooms dedicated to student choice.

Even with early resistance to growing a culture of classroom choice, students desire choice. Once choice is a comfortable part of the culture, it breeds happiness, playfulness, and creativity. It allows students to link learning together and begin to see the context for learning. Choice allows learning to layer, and it provides a place for ideas to emerge, the kind of ideas that never emerge in a tightly prescriptive environment. Feeling the power that student choice brings to the classroom is often the catapult that a teacher needs to take additional steps forward as a connected educator and classroom leader.

THE CLASSROOM CONNECTION

Bill Powers leads an excellent staff of middle school teachers in Springfield, Missouri. His story is one about growing choice through collaboration and trust. It is about building a culture for learning and allowing his staff to grow from the inside out. Bill leads by example, and he has been a great asset to the growth of leaders throughout the state. Enjoy how he shares with pride about the beautiful work being done by his teachers for the students at his school. As connected teachers and teacher leaders, they experience incredible new growth in their roles.

Used with permission from Bill Powers.

More than three years ago, I took a journey with Twitter and became @MrPowersCMS. During my time learning, growing, and connecting on Twitter, I have been stretched to think differently and see differently. One topic of interest is student choice and voice. Recently I took the time to visit with approximately 100 students during lunch to ask them about their favorite teachers and what characteristics made them great educators.

"Someone who is funny and makes learning fun," one student said. When digging further, the students described this as someone who enjoyed teaching and allowed it to show in their day-to-day interactions with students. "They laugh with us when we make mistakes, and they aren't always uptight about every little thing." A few students went on to say, "We make mistakes. We are kids. It's not that we don't care. We do care, and we really are trying." Several students continued, "They (teachers) remember what it is like to be a kid, and they don't take everything so seriously."

One student said he learned best from "someone who really cares about me." Basically the overall perception of students was they can tell the difference between "lip service" and genuine caring. Several students said they felt insulted by teachers who "pretend" to care about them. Relationships matter. We know this, and some educators have a knack for connecting with students. At our school, a few teachers found another way to strengthen the classroom connection through the student choice that comes from flipped learning.

By building connections with great educators across the country, I now have a growing culture of taking risks and failing forward. By failing forward, I mean creating the conditions for kids to made mistakes, learn from their mistakes, and continuously reflect and think about their learning over time by adjusting the factors that influence it. My thought was always, "What do we have to lose?" Two teachers began to experiment by introducing video clips and lectures via video to better use class time for student choice opportunities. The next summer, we were able to send them to a flipped learning conference to connect with other educators from across the country.

One of those teachers, Lindsay Wright said, "I am always looking for ideas to help my students learn. We are presented with so many different strategies that will help certain groups of students, but I'm always searching for models that will help all. By flipping my classroom, I can now spend the entire class time helping students on concepts with which they are struggling. Right now, flipping my classroom is working great, but I am always looking for the next great things."

Wright's students and families often share how much they appreciate the videos, as it allows them to fast-forward through concepts they know but also rewind and review other concepts with which they may struggle or those they need to review. Others have stated how they now enjoy math again because of having new confidence, a confidence that comes from having greater access to the teacher during class and choices about how to access the videos (smart phone, tablet, or computer).

Another innovative way we are providing our students choice is through Genius Hour or 20% Time. Genius Hour, or 20%, provides time during the school day for students to pursue ideas, concepts, and areas of learning about which they are passionate. I learned about this idea after reading Daniel Pink's book *Drive*. I shared some of my thoughts with staff at team meetings, faculty meetings, and during one-on-one conversations. Three of our staff members embarked on adding this opportunity of voice and choice for students. This was a perfect way to allow our students to learn through choice. One student said, "We don't all have the same talents, but we all have something to offer to the class. In most of my classes, we are all expected to do the same thing."

The students mentioned that they enjoyed having a choice and hands-on activities. Another student noted, "Some teachers enjoy hearing themselves talk too much. I can Google most of what they tell me." When I asked more probing questions, the students continued by saying, "I want to learn by doing, not by writing down facts that I will never need." Another teacher, Angela Starns, said, "Genius Hour gives students the opportunity to choose to learn exactly what they want to learn, how to learn it, and how to show the learning. Taking a project from an idea to a finished project with few limitations or guidelines can be a daunting task for students, but it is an experience that mirrors real life. Students are constantly approaching me with a problem or question, and while I offer guidance, I always remind them the decision is theirs. The choices that they make then impact what happens next in the project. Students figure out really quickly the product of Genius Hour really depends on the effort they expend. I like that the responsibility of learning is placed on the students' shoulders."

Starns notes the feedback from parents and students has been positive and even in the face of failure students are learning. "While my students may not be completing the most elaborate projects, they are often unaware of the many things that they are learning while completing their Genius Hour projects."

Kristen Wilson also decided to give Genius Hour a shot. "What an incredible opportunity to help students realize they can learn about anything. In the information age, they don't have to wait to be spoon fed information to learn. Because the point was to give students the opportunity to discover they were capable of teaching themselves, I allowed a wide range of projects, such as arts and crafts, research, design, languages, and cooking."

This opportunity to branch out, take risks, and understand failure without fear has allowed several of our staff members to provide students with nontraditional options for learning. It allowed students a voice in their learning and also a choice in what they learned, how they learned, and how to show mastery. Unfortunately, many of our schools and classrooms still resemble the ones we attended as students—desks in a neat rows and the teachers as the sole provider of information. Through a shift in mindset and taking risks, we now have teachers beginning their journey as connected educators.

"I decided to take this risk because schools are changing—classrooms are changing—the way students learn is changing," Wilson said. "I wanted the opportunity to make learning more engaging for my students, while better preparing them for a world in which they will have to think critically and navigate all of the information that is at their fingertips."

ACTION STEPS

1. ***Choose something small.** There may be 10 minutes at the end of a week when students get to choose their learning path. Grab ahold of this time, and shape this into something special. Choice is an odd concept for kids early in the process, but using small chunks of time can make the transition a bit easier for teachers and students.
2. **Speak up on something easy.** It is difficult to break the habit of silence. As a connected educator, it is important to ask the questions that need to be asked. This can happen in a small group meetings, department meetings, or faculty meetings. Attempt to say something that makes the group uncomfortable. It is a great step for moving from congenial to collegial.
3. **Flip something.** Can you make a video that helps kids learn? It doesn't need to be a lecture or an inspiring video, but something recorded that can help kids learn. Recording a video is as easy as ever, and it brings learning to students in a format they enjoy.
4. **Think about choice in process and product.** Student choice can exist in a variety of places in the learning process. It can exist at the beginning of the learning path where students choose their own ideas to learn. It can exist in the process where students choose the road to the same final project, or choice can emerge in the end product that showcases the student learning.

RESOURCES

These links provide two great videos that can be used with students as well as adults to begin the conversation about what the culture of a connected classroom should feel like and look like. Also, it is worth looking at the flipped classroom infographic as it outlines the important elements of a successful flipped classroom and, when done correctly, how it can positively impact engagement and achievement.

Dan Pink on Taking Risks (https://www.youtube.com/watch?v=VOU6zoRI3BU)

Ten Expectations in Learning (https://www.youtube.com/watch?v=K96c-TGnSf4)

The Flipped Classroom Infographic (http://www.knewton.com/wp-content/uploads/flipped-classroom-short1.png)

CHAPTER 3

A Passion for Learning

Not unlike a maple tree tapped for its syrup, many spaces of learning are draining their students of the beauty that resides in their soul for learning.

ESSENTIAL QUESTIONS

1. How can passion lie at the heart of learning?
2. In what ways can you reignite learning in the students who struggle to be motivated?
3. Who was the teacher who grew the passion for learning inside you? What lessons could be taken from this person?

THE THEORY

Watching young learners wilt is one of the most difficult things for passionate educators. Learners enter school eager, with a genuine beauty, in their desire to learn. They ask questions. They make meaning. They construct paths for their knowledge to fit together. Slowly, and mostly without notice, the passion of learning is sucked out of these young minds. In school after school, and in classroom after classroom, the fuel that keeps these young minds sharp and eager is slowly removed from the system. It is a rare classroom where play and passion remain in the forefront throughout the K–12 experience. In many places, it starts with worksheets and homework that have little to do with building skills, knowledge, or application. It extends to a grading system that focuses only on point gathering. It begins to pull the arts, physical education, science, and social studies from an equal standing with other areas of learning. It has students buried in textbooks, and the opportunities to work outside the normal become a way of the past. None of this happens all at once, but at a rate and pace that isn't noticed by students, parents, or the community.

The end of this process is a series of meetings where five to ten educational professionals sit in a room to develop a new plan of action for the students because the students are at risk of failing. They are showing no interest in school. They aren't completing their work. They are missing school, and they aren't engaged in the lessons during class. Many intelligent professionals sit in the room with binders and folders of data around the latest way to encourage students to reengage with a system that is chronically failing its students. After many meetings, nothing sustainable is usually in place, and the engagement of these students is often lost for a lifetime.

These students, for which these meetings are conducted, go on to tell stories about how they hated school. They say that it didn't help them get a job, find a career, or build happiness in their life. Why did it spiral to this point? How did the five-year-old child who had an innate love of learning become the lead story about how kids fail? There is certainly no single moment that creates these situations, but buried in the details is a slow loss of passion in the classroom caused by structures, routines, laws, and assumptions that cause teachers and classrooms to transition learning away from its natural form and, in turn, mold an unhealthy recipe for kids.

Connected classrooms are different, and they exist in schools across the United States. The teachers who fill these rooms aren't rare, but there is certainly a need for more. Joining the coalition of the willing surrounding connected classrooms means finding time to nurture the passions of the students through resources, space, and energy. Students need to know how important it is for them to learn without grades, points, and other external motivation factors. They need to know there is power and possibility in their passions.

When students are allowed time to learn about the things that spark their interest, some naturally beautiful things occur. Kids look forward to learning. They make connections between their work and the learning that is happening in other areas. Students begin to look for new places to grow and learn. At times, this can be scary and unnerving for teachers, as another piece of control is drawn away from the teacher and pushed into the purview of the student. It also creates tension about curriculum coverage, the perspectives of colleagues and supervisors about how instructional time is being used, and the impression of parents, but the courageous connected classroom leader recognizes the essential nature of this work around building passion in all students and maintaining the five-year-old child's desire for learning and growth.

THE CLASSROOM CONNECTION

Laura Gilchrist, a cultivator of minds and souls in Kansas City, shared her story about why she ripped the posters off her wall. It is a story of how inspiration from her professional learning network fed her desire for fresh student creation. Since that moment, Laura has unleashed the passion of kids in their learning through projects and partnerships. She inspires kids and other educators with her extreme desire to share and support learning in all places around the planet.

Used with permission from Laura Gilchrist.

It was convocation day in my school district, and I was excited to hear the story our keynote speaker, Darren Kuropatwa, had to share with us. Darren is a digital learning consultant and a curriculum coordinator in Canada. He believes wholeheartedly in the transformative power of visual storytelling for learners of all ages. What made this keynote speech so powerful and awesome for me was that I already "knew" Darren. You see, I was already connected to Darren's ideas, thoughts, and pictures via Twitter, Flickr, and Instagram. He was in my personal learning network or PLN.

The big "stories" of his keynote were nothing new or earth shattering, but they were bold and exciting. They struck a chord with me. Since about 80% of your brain is set up to process visual information in the form of pictures and videos, and since being in charge of your own learning is the best way to learn and grow, the task for us as educators is clear. We should give kids the tools and the time to learn, create, and analyze all things visual in their days at school.

We should make visual learning a priority, on equal footing with text. We should allow and teach kids to glean information from pictures and, on the flip side, create pictures and other visual products to share learning, ideas, and stories. Put the kids in charge, give them the tools, and get out of the way.

During his time on our stage, Darren had us take out our phones and participate. It was great fun. He had us take a selfie from our seats in the audience, download the Phonto app, and then add some text to the picture. He then shared his Flickr e-mail address, and asked us to send our pictures to that address. Our pictures popped up on his Flickr account. They were our pictures and our thoughts, all together in one place for our viewing. They were powerful. How could only a few words and a picture convey so much meaning? It was a new way of thinking. I got to participate, and my ideas and views mattered. It was learner centered and empowering.

I took Darren's message and inspiration to heart and crafted a project to get the kids immersed in visual learning. I ripped the posters off the walls. Other people created them. Why couldn't the kids create their own posters? I started what I called my "Our Walls, Our Posters" iPad/Flickr Project with my sixth graders. Here's how the lesson unfolded. The iPads were out on the tables and kids could use their cell phones. My Flickr e-mail address was on the board. Science concepts we'd been working on and some inspirational quotes and links were on the board as well. Most important, the walls were bare.

My challenge to the kids: Splash these walls with your paint! Create your own posters with your work, ideas, and pictures in them. Add minimal text to get the point across. E-mail your posters to my Flickr e-mail address, and we'll work together to decorate our room. We will create instead of consume, and we will focus on pictures to convey rich thoughts with minimal text.

The kids accepted the challenge as worthy and noble and set off with great fervor, finding PhotoBooth on the iPad, a keen source of inspiration and possibility. Kids worked alone or in groups to flesh out their idea for theme, text, and picture. They took pictures with people or objects in them, or they took pictures of art they'd created on paper or whiteboard. The kids, using the iPads, added text to the pictures in Keynote and Pages. The kids, using cell phones, used apps such as Phonto to add text to their pictures. I could also add text to any picture right inside of Flickr using its built-in photo editor, Aviary. The scene in the classroom, as pictures started flying into my Flickr account, was one of hushed excitement. The kids huddled near the projector screen, and we watched the pictures pop up on my Flickr page. Their faces lit up when they saw their very own work appear on the screen. After we printed them at the poster printer and laminated them, the posters were proudly attached to our walls. The kids loved seeing their faces and ideas around them. I can't wait to see the classroom walls at the end of the school year and experience the feeling of being surrounded by their work and their pictures. One student made a tantalizing comment as a result of this experience. He said we should do this same thing throughout the school. We should cover all the walls with posters and pictures that we created.

ACTION STEPS

1. ***Do something that sparks your passion for learning.** Not sure if this means going to an art fair, playing golf, or listening to live music, but if you, as a teacher, aren't pursuing your passion, then you will always struggle to unleash the passion of your students. Truly experience something that brings you joy and soak in the feelings that come from the experience.
2. ***Figuratively tear something off the walls.** Change is hard, but change doesn't start with incremental moves in the right direction. It starts with a moment. What moment will cause you to jump in the pool of connected educators? When you "tear something off the walls?" When you do, you will feel liberated, scared, and more. Enjoy the emotion, and then focus on how the change will impact kids.
3. **Ask kids what matters to them.** It is amazing how often we *do* learning to kids. The voice of our students should be shaping our work on a daily basis. The kids don't get to decide everything, but they should get to decide a lot more in a connected classroom. Passion for learning is an incredible opportunity that so many teachers are leaving on the sidelines.

4. **Take the long view.** Working in education is a complex task, and it requires seasoning. It would be great to save every kid in the first year and never leave a child behind. In the first few years of teaching you believe that you are reaching every kid; until five years later, you realized that you were reaching none of them. It takes a long time to be a great teacher, but meanwhile, be a really good one, and never stop trying to be a great one.

RESOURCES

Growing students' desire to learn and their passionate drive for change and advocacy is at the heart of the connected classroom. Use these links to explore three different sets of information that can chart the course of a classroom to a more passion-filled place of learning. Focus closely on the essential tenets of passion-based learning described by Angela Maiers.

Being a Passionate Educator Begins and Ends With Cybrary Man's Collections (http://cybraryman.com/passionbasedlearning.html)

Angela Maiers Showcases the Power of Passion-Based Learning (http://www.angelamaiers.com/2011/07/guidelines-of-passion-based-learning.html)

More on the concept of Genius Hour (http://www.geniushour.com/)

CHAPTER 4

Knowing the Core of Your Learning

To provide student choice, it is essential to know the depth of your standards and curriculum.

ESSENTIAL QUESTIONS

1. When you boil your philosophy of education into a tweet, what is left?
2. How do we keep curriculum alive and vibrant?
3. In what ways can we build systems to pass institutional excellence to new people in the organization?

THE THEORY

What matters in education is a vibrant and ongoing conversation. It allows education to stay fresh and relevant, and it defies the idea that a decision has been made about what is essential in learning forever. Couple these conversations with the new rate of information flow and it makes it very hard to blend the perfect content for students. Running in parallel with this challenge around content is the deep need to create space for personalized learning to allow for the growth of the heads, hearts, and souls of all learners. In many places, standards, curriculum, and units are written, and before the ink is dry, they are outdated as the best resources, materials, and ideas are evolving minute by minute.

The rate of change around best practices in curriculum, instruction, and assessment make it difficult for any teacher to truly know what should be at the core of the learning taking place in the classroom.

Some classrooms that have followed a backward-design approach can speak to the enduring understandings and essential questions embedded in the units as the core, while others will point to the standards passed down from local, state, or federal officials as central to their work. Standards, enduring understandings, and essential questions all provide some guidance about the core learning of a classroom, but rarely are these right-sized for teachers to allow an agile connected classroom that can take advantage of learning opportunities that emerge in the moment.

Knowing the core is one of the most essential pieces of the connected classroom. It is one of the jewels for veteran teachers, and these teachers rarely know that they even know the wisdom of the core. It allows them to not stress about coverage and relax around the fact that learning bled over into another period. These teachers know the core items that leverage the most learning from their students. Being a successful connected educator requires wisdom, a wisdom that comes from quality conversations with the other educators around the country seeking the same clarity. Pursuing this, and eventually achieving this clarity, brings incredible advantages to students because these connected teachers are no longer leading instruction like the other classrooms, but instead, they are in rhythm with their learners. Keeping curriculum alive, meaningful, and relevant means knowing it, owning it, and designing it until the core emerges and it connects seamlessly to the educational philosophy of the connected classroom leader.

THE CLASSROOM CONNECTION

Julie Szaj has an opportunity to grow educators throughout Missouri and beyond in the art and science of teaching. Her story speaks the truth about how difficult excellent teaching really is. She identifies how knowing yourself as a teacher is often an overlooked piece of the journey of an excellent classroom leader. She pushes educators to grow into the type of teacher that kids, ten years from now, will need. Julie makes a compelling argument for adding the tools of reflection into the practice of the connected educator.

Teaching is complicated. It doesn't matter if you are instructing a group of squirrely first graders, a hormone-filled cluster of middle schoolers, or a band of striving-to-be-independent high schoolers, our profession is faced with the challenge of trying to keep up in a world that does not stand still. How do we accommodate the constant changes? How do we meet the needs of a demanding curriculum and testing routine while still valuing our students and their learning styles? In my opinion, it all comes down to fully understanding your curriculum and how it has evolved in this new era of learning.

In today's classroom, it is no longer acceptable for students to simply memorize facts for a multiple-choice test. Teachers can no longer be satisfied with basic, brief explanations of learning found in typical textbooks. Instead, teachers must present students with a problem, allow them to identify and grapple with the complex underlying issues, and guide the learning process along the way. For this to happen, there must be a shift of thinking in education. We must teach for understanding, not for grades or test scores.

So how do we begin? You can start by taking a fresh look at your curriculum. Look at it like you have never seen it before, and examine it with a critical eye geared toward finding the important stuff, the real stuff. Look at it and ask yourself, "Why do my students need to know this?" Is this content something that has "always been taught" or is it a concept that will allow your students to become contributors to a society that is steeped in culture, values, and diversity. Once you find those key concepts and ideas, this is where you will start building learning experiences, the experiences that take your students into a lifetime filled with curiosity and a love for learning.

Look at what you have identified. What natural connections do you see? Reflect on your life and the lives of others you know. Consider what is happening in the world today, in the present, all over the world. What specifically do we need to know, understand, and be able to do to function on a daily basis? What prerequisite skills are needed to be able to tackle the "big ideas" that are thrown our way? How might your core concepts be combined to help your students through life?

While the previous reflection is not easy, it is necessary. If teachers do not understand why they are teaching a specific skill or concept, how can you expect students to understand why they need to learn it?

Now that you have identified your core curriculum, it is time to contemplate how to best share it so students can build connections and meaning from the content. This is where the craft of teaching comes into play. Without knowledge of pedagogy, everything can quickly fall apart. It starts with knowing the students.

How well do I really know the students? Do you know what activities they enjoy outside of school? Do you know the students' parents? Have you ever spoken to the students on a personal level about things that matter to them? Have you ever envisioned what it might be like to be them just for one day or night? If you answer no to these questions, ask yourself, "Why not?" More important, decide what you are going to do about it.

You see, to teach students anything, you have to know them first. You have to know what makes them tick so you can structure your teaching to meet them exactly where they are in the moment. Take a look at what you know, and you can combine the needs of the students with proven pedagogy and teaching strategies to meet the needs of the core of the curriculum. In addition, consider how the students are going to demonstrate their learning. How might they take advantage of their strengths and abilities? What choices might they have? Consider creating a rubric or assessment tool that will allow for multiple types of products and stay focused on assessing the standards and skills.

Dedicate time to truly reflect on your core curriculum, teaching practices, and the needs of your students. Focus your efforts on ways to give your students a voice and choice, and build a culture of curiosity, wonderment, and risk taking. Know your curriculum deeply, know your students in new ways, and above all, engage your students in the real learning that they deserve.

ACTION STEPS

1. **Black out the rest.** Our curriculum coverage isn't fair. The amount of stuff we are asked to teach creates pressure and expectations that aren't achievable. New teachers take on the challenge and succeed in coverage, veteran teachers throw a lot away without a

true plan, and those in the middle ponder how to make it work. Connected classrooms will never be successful until we are deleters by design. Take a marker and say no by design to the things that won't be a part of this year's work.

2. ***tweet your class.** Can you explain the purpose of your course in 140 characters? This is a great opportunity to get to the core of the course. It means truly explaining to a larger audience that your very complex classroom does have a simple narrative even if it isn't the entire story of what you do. Too often educators can't explain their course and its content to someone else. This makes it impossible for common conversation.
3. ***End binder mentality.** For the sake of all curriculum writers, remove your curriculum from a binder. It is better to be written on a bar napkin than in a binder. So many of our attempts to build curriculum end up on shelves without any impact. All curriculum needs to be open, transparent, and ready for the next iteration by adults or kids.
4. **Talk about your work.** Facilitators of learning in classrooms are notorious for telling the wrong stories. It is so easy to tell the story about the student who causes stress while 90% of students are going about their business in a way that would make everyone proud. Teachers need to share and talk about their work so that those outside of education grow their understanding about what really matters in education.

RESOURCES

There is great beauty in providing student voice into classrooms and communities. Both of the projects linked here as well as the focus on student voice and presenting in the Common Core Standards provide incredible guidance and inspiration on how to bring greater voice to the connected classroom.

One World Youth Project (http://oneworldyouthproject.org/)

Story Corps—National Teachers Initiative (http://storycorps.org/national-teachers/)

Common Core Standards (http://www.corestandards.org/)

CHAPTER 5

Learning That I Never Expected

Providing student choice often brings unexpected learning that goes well beyond expectations.

ESSENTIAL QUESTIONS

1. What are the best ways to allow deeper learning to emerge?
2. How do prescriptive assignments limit creativity in classrooms?
3. What kinds of learning happen in your classroom that have nothing to do with your teaching?

THE THEORY

Liberty allows us the freedom needed for creativity to flourish, solutions to percolate, and the best choices to emerge. Allowing students who are learning how to best make choices the opportunities to choose can be a very uncomfortable place for many classrooms. This freedom is ripe for mistakes and messiness, not the hallmarks of most contemporary learning spaces. The best classrooms are finding ways to move beyond the traditional amount of choice to a more robust choice menu for students. This menu includes choice around what to study, how to study it, and also how to showcase it for a larger audience.

Growth through choice comes in many flavors. One piece comes from learning how to choose. Students are going to make mistakes, and they are going to make bad choices. Often, these poor choices come from a lack of practice and reflection on how to make choices as opposed to a willful desire to negatively impact others with the choices. Allowing failure in choice in schools creates a safer place to fail along with space to reflect and improve. Through this iterative process, students grow as choosers. They begin to build a set of tools and decision-making protocols, whether formal or informal, that allow them to take more actions by design.

There is fresh learning and growth that comes with choice. When students have a chance to choose how they want to showcase their learning, they build capacity around owning their decisions and bringing their ideas from infancy to completion. Students with choice also learn that it can change in the middle of a situation because of resource, human, or emotional needs. They begin to see that choice isn't the end of the decision-making process, but the beginning. Once choice is a part of the DNA of a classroom, it breeds more choices. The students are learning both the freedom of choice and the balance of choice in a safe, reflective environment.

Choice is a cornerstone to the connected classroom. It requires classroom leaders with the courage to abandon full control and substitute it with full learning; full learning that brings smiles, playfulness, and joy back to the classroom.

THE CLASSROOM CONNECTION

Kristy Daniels-Jackson serves the students of the Webster Groves School District in Saint Louis as the coordinator of gifted education. Her story speaks to fostering creativity for all students. Her passion for creativity has allowed her the opportunity to plan incredible learning opportunities for kids to pursue their learning passions. Kristy looks for ways to support positive risk to achieve moments of deep learning.

Used with permission from Kristy Daniels-Jackson.

Many gifted students can perform intellectual tasks, but creativity and risk taking don't always come as easily for them. Over the years, I have observed many gifted students and adults who were highly intelligent but lacked the motivation, tenacity, or fortitude to be highly successful in life. This issue has become my mission. I am determined to find and create opportunities that allow students and adults to engage in creative thinking and risk taking.

I began looking for opportunities to promote creativity within my professional network. I made a connection with my colleague Dr. Steve Coxon, assistant professor of gifted education at Maryville University and director of the Maryville Young Scholars Program. Dr. Coxon is a true friend and resource to the gifted education community. He invited me to present for the teacher training component of the program. The Maryville Young Scholars Program provides a state and national model for increasing diversity in gifted education programs so that all children have the opportunity to reach their potential, regardless of family background. This opportunity would allow me to share with teachers creative-thinking strategies that they could utilize in their classrooms. We explored strategies for cultivating parallel thinking with Ed Debono's six thinking hats. The beauty of the six hats strategy is that it can be used for creative problem solving in any environment. Debono uses colored hats as a metaphor for each distinct area of thinking. The idea is to lessen the unnatural feeling of "putting on" a different way of thinking. The six areas of thinking are listed here:

- Information (white hat)—considering what are the facts?
- Emotions (red hat)—intuitive or instinctive statements of emotional feeling
- Discernment (black hat)—identifying reasons to be cautious and conservative
- Define the Focus (blue hat)—focus on the subject: what is our goal?
- Optimistic response (yellow hat)—identifying benefits, seeking harmony
- Creativity (green hat)—provocation and investigation, what if?

The work with Maryville and the six hat strategy has carried over to my current role as the curriculum coordinator of gifted education in the Webster Groves School District. This responsibility allows me the opportunity to support a team of dedicated gifted specialists. My leadership style is collaborative; therefore, I work to ensure a safe space for specialists to create and take risks. This empowers them to create solutions that benefit the students and our learning community. One solution that emerged was the creation of our districtwide Creative Challenge Day. Although our district is not extremely large, we still found it difficult for our students to get to know one another and collaborate across the six elementary schools.

We looked at this challenge as an opportunity for our team to take a risk and do something we have never done. This issue became the spark that led to Creative Challenge Day. After months of planning, scheduling, and advocating for the event, the first Creative Challenge Day took place. The day was designed to engage students in high-level thinking in a friendly competitive environment that involves teamwork, task organization, idea generation, democratic process, and decision making. Students worked in teams to design solutions to various problem-based learning challenges that included building a green amusement park with recycled materials and a crack-proof egg container.

In the end, we learned that getting out of the way when kids are engaged is much harder than bringing out their creativity. The day provided hundreds of choice opportunities for kids and a safe place to practice choosing. Creative Challenge Day is now an annual event. When I reflect on this work, it becomes obvious that giving others the time, space, and opportunity to take a risk and choose wisely yields outcomes that were never expected.

ACTION STEPS

1. **Break the rules.** Many teachers achieve their level of status by following the rules and doing school the right way. To find the courage to lead a connected classroom, it requires looking for ways to break the rules to support kids in their learning. Break the rules for the right reason. Paint your walls. Burn a candle. Bring in a refrigerator. Connected educators grow in their ability to ask for forgiveness as opposed to asking for permission.

2. ***Create time for creativity.** Creating doesn't happen without space and time. In a world consumed with itself every moment of every day, it is hard to find time to breathe, let alone be creative. Schedule time for making, drawing, coloring, and more. Creativity spawns itself in the smallest moments, but as classroom demands grow, creativity is being elbowed out.
3. **Make the stuff for the best kids, the stuff for all kids.** I'm not sure who decided that the learning strategies of gifted education needed to be contained to a tiny percentage of our population, but the good stuff is the good stuff, and all of our students should have access to best practices every day. It is hard to imagine that the most engaging ways of learning are trapped in classrooms with only our brightest students. Do the fun, engaging, exciting, and energizing stuff with everyone because it grows deep learning.
4. ****Choosing lunch shouldn't be *the* choice moment of the day.** Students need to feel in control of their learning. The other 18 hours of kids' lives are more hectic than ever, so school needs to be a place where kids are in control of their learning. For too many students, the only choice at school that they make comes at lunch—chicken, pizza, or hamburgers. How do we make our classroom a place of choice? Is it about seats? Is it about students using their phones? Is it about how they showcase their learning?

RESOURCES

The two TED talks in this set of links provide a great way to start conversations about injecting creativity into the classroom. In addition, there is fantastic information about deeper learning and how to make time and space in the classroom for students to reflect and dig into the topics about which they are passionate.

Sir Ken Robinson—How Schools Kill Creativity (http://www.ted.com/talks/ken_robinson_says_schools_kill_creativity)

Amy Tan—Where Does Creativity Hide (http://www.ted.com/talks/amy_tan_on_creativity)

The Importance of Deeper Learning (http://www.hewlett.org/programs/education/deeper-learning)

CHAPTER 6

From the Mouths of Babes

As we provide students voice, many truths emerge.

ESSENTIAL QUESTIONS

1. How has your classroom teaching shifted to maximize engagement?
2. Where is the fine line between control and being controlling for teachers?
3. How do we allow our students to contribute more deeply to the classroom conversation?

THE THEORY

Having students at the edge of their seats and leaning into the learning is a beautiful moment for any teacher. No matter whether it is a finely tuned unit of study that has students working in groups to solve a real-world problem or a moment when the teacher is telling a story, it is in those moments of engagement that the art and science of teaching come together. Teachers remember and savor these moments as they are the moments that keep their belly fire for teaching stoked. Creating these moments isn't a matter of chance or serendipity; they come from finely tuned instructional practices that allow the learning to flow.

At the heart of this work, in the best classrooms with the best classroom leaders, is a focus on the power of voice. In early learning, students are eager to participate and share their ideas. They are leaning into learning without the need for technology, classroom management tricks, or cooperative learning strategies. They know that their voice is important, and their learning flourishes. Our youngest learners feel the power of their voice grow, and they support the voices of the others. As students get older, many factors begin to drain this desire to learn. Some of it is an awareness of their peers. This awareness creates a reluctance to look stupid, and it keeps students from leaning into their learning at the level necessary to grow deeply. Another factor is classroom culture. A culture of control begins to grow in many classrooms as each grade level passes. This can look like an increased desire for less talking in the classroom, more rules and procedures to control the flow of conversation, and a growing amount of the teacher at the front of the room to control the pace and speed of learning. This need for control, or perceived control, leads to more and more students learning that to do well in school, it is necessary to talk less, "play school," and make sure that their voice isn't the one heard above the rest.

This leads to a cascade of events that lowers interest in learning and begins to remove the passion and engagement from classrooms. As these control factors are what are valued by the teacher, the students begin to police themselves by applying additional peer pressure to comply in the classroom. Students who speak up now are seen as the nerds, know-it-alls, and the teacher's pets. The students who persevere through this pressure can find great rewards as they grow into lifelong learners, but too many students wilt from the peer pressure, and they find themselves looking for other avenues beyond school where their voice is heard. They look for ways to become invisible in classrooms, and they begin to build a tool chest of ways to avoid looking academic. This armor builds educational plaque that causes decay in the quantity and quality of learning that is taking place.

Connected classrooms work to fend off this disease. They build a culture where it is cool to learn, ask questions, and be a top performer. Teachers in these spaces are able to reward the right behavior, use the right praise, and address the little digs that erode the desire to learn for students. All of these efforts validate the power of individual student voice. Connected classrooms can fight the trend of fading engagement. They keep kids connected and build a desire for learning that lasts no matter the pressure, inertia, or trends pushing back from the outside.

THE CLASSROOM CONNECTION

Kathy Bellew served as the technology director in a small rural school district outside Saint Louis. In this role, she had an opportunity to see great learning and to help shape and scale innovation and best practice. Her story is one of failing forward in an attempt to amplify voice and classroom engagement. It is about growing from mistakes and being persistent in the face of adversity. Kathy makes things happen, and the students in her school district reap many rewards from her vision to give every kid the learning opportunities and experiences that they deserve.

A decision was made by the Grandview R-II School District to proceed with a 1:1 mobile environment in the high school. We would provide devices for every student, and I was charged with the task to make it happen. Thus began my investigation that would include infrastructure upgrades, device discovery and piloting, policy changes, and implementation. Grandview resides in a rural area where many students do not have Internet at home; therefore, we would need to ensure that students could have everything delivered to their device before leaving school for the day. With the support of administration and the board of education, it became a daunting project that fell on the shoulders of the media specialist and me.

Our initial thought was to start with the most basic level of success. Every student would have digital textbooks and access to the Internet, and we would provide e-books in our library that would help us with our state standards. It didn't take very long, though, to realize that we were attaining so much more than that. I had the fortune of being in the chemistry teacher's classroom when he remarked to the students, "You are getting the benefit of a secondary education." He wasn't just referring to the use of computers, but to the type of learning that would be taking place from the delivery of material, to the problem solving, to the collaboration and research.

Many students asked if they could bring their own device because it was either better than what we provided or they were more comfortable with a device with which they were more familiar. We leaned into the choice as we listened to the students' thoughts and ideas on the topic. Even with great planning and student voice in the process, the first year was a near failure. Device hardware failures and breakage plagued the program, and the deaths of three students and one teacher rocked the entire school culture and any momentum that there may have been. We learned a lot in that first year.

We reevaluated the program, made changes, and had an opportunity to reset for year two. The biggest insight came as people surrounding the program realized that providing a device for student learning was really providing a device for student-*centered* learning. Students were actually gaining control of their education through the opportunity to have this device. We began to reshape our processes surrounding student-centered learning.

We were changing the standard teaching methods into more connected ways of learning. Using cloud storage and availability of online programs, we had more collaboration projects, and teachers gained more flexibility with their instruction through online resources and open-source textbooks. We also offered virtual courses that enabled students across the state to participate, and we offered courses not typically included in the traditional school year.

During all of the change, we supported teachers with the needed training to shift the way that they helped students learn. We needed to show them things such as how to physically rearrange their classrooms and modify the content of their lessons to reflect a change in instruction. We also needed to train students. Students needed to learn about digital citizenship and responsibility, and our hope was to provide them with the foundation to be successful and contribute to society in a positive and responsible manner.

Are students engaged? Oh yes, most definitely. Are they engaged in the lessons we are providing to them? Not always, but isn't that part of the process? Part of our challenge is to instruct students on appropriate use of technology and to help them find the time and a place for chatting and playing games. Learning should be fun. Students and teachers alike should *want* to learn, grow, develop, and be engaged. Grandview is a progressive school that has found a good fit for technology in the day-to-day classroom. Students will benefit by becoming more technology literate, developing problem-solving skills, learning to work together, and developing goals. We will instruct them in ways to work collaboratively, be responsible, and take control of their learning that should take them well beyond their K–12 experience.

ACTION STEPS

1. ***Make mistakes out loud.** Kids need to see us as fallible. They need to know how we deal with mistakes. Connected educators talk through their mistakes and failures publicly to connect kids to the process of processing through issues. Kids in these cultures are more apt to take chances with their learning.
2. **Teach the art of conversation.** The norms around conversation vary from household to household and from community to community, but as the global classroom blossoms and kids are interacting with more adults in their learning, it is essential that we are building the skills of excellent conversation. This includes individual, small group, and large group conversations.
3. **Begin the conversation about better 1:1 opportunities.** Even the most technology rich schools are often poor in their technology integration. As a teacher, your voice matters to leaders throughout the district. Make sure to advocate for the true needs of your students in the realm of technology. Too many devices are purchased without student and teacher voice, and it equals poor results.
4. ***Notice serendipity.** When the learning of a unit that is taking place in the classroom connects to an e-mail or an article that you are reading, it isn't by chance, but it is an opportunity. When a student brings up a topic, and it links to previous learning, lean in. The greatest moments of a teaching career come in courageous moments when we chase the rabbit into the hole and beauty emerges.

RESOURCES

The art of teaching remains an essential element for the connected classroom. Teachers can enrich learning in incredible ways by seizing the opportunities that come from student ideas, current ideas, and noticing the world beyond the classroom. Tools such as Socratic Seminar, the tools of Clarity from Bright Bytes and the wisdom of TED talks all can play a role in creating a more deeply connected classroom.

Using Socratic Seminar (http://www.readwritethink.org/professional-development/strategy-guides/socratic-seminars-30600.html)

Clarity from Bright Bytes—Measuring Technology Integration (http://brightbytes.net/)

Losing Serendipity—A TED Talk (https://www.youtube.com/watch?v=5p0VK_-BoJI)

CHAPTER 7

Everyone Listens to a Kid

As adults fail to listen to one another respectfully, there is always room for the voice of a student.

ESSENTIAL QUESTIONS

1. How can students be our best consultants for classroom innovation?
2. What value is there to share classroom ownership with kids?
3. How does classroom design impact the ability for students to be heard?

THE THEORY

School leaders and teacher leaders are often looking for wisdom about how to improve instruction. They will travel to conferences, listen to keynote speakers, search for online resources, stream TED talks, and pay consultants searching for that chunk of wisdom that improves the learning in the classroom. Often, these leaders will also visit other schools, do book studies, and have parent focus groups to discuss how to build a more engaging classroom. There is much wisdom to be gained from being connected to other educators in all of these spaces, but there is wisdom much closer to home that is overlooked. The wisdom of the students provides an opportunity for new levels of learning—if the adults are willing to build a school culture where students are an equal part of the planning and implementation of the processes necessary for school excellence.

Student voice changes everything. In some learning spaces, this emerges from classroom meetings and Socratic seminars that discuss the best ways that students can learn, but eventually, these events to include voice need to become more systemic. Designing excellent classrooms, where students are engaged and excited in their work, requires empathy for students that comes from listening.

Student voice can be a part of most adult meetings that take place in schools. Imagine bringing students to faculty meetings to participate as equals. In so many places, this would completely change the tone and energy level at those meetings. Imagine students being called in to conversations around purchasing and master scheduling, and gathering feedback on grading policies, testing, and how to craft afterschool activities for the learners. The insights available in all of these situations are tremendous, yet most educators leave this untapped wisdom on the sidelines—out of habit, arrogance, or laziness.

When students begin to feel heard, there is a shift in ownership surrounding learning. Students begin to feel less like school is being done to them and more that they are cocreators in the process. Once students put on the cloak that comes with the role of cocreator, more truths about their needs as learners emerge. As connected teachers and leaders, there are opportunities to take feedback and open dialogue in a digital, asynchronous space as well. This can include things such as Google Forms, comments on a student blog, or having students create video portfolios.

Voice is an opportunity for a continuous feedback cycle. It is saying that as adults we value the young minds that enter the doors. Listening to the voice of students can also expose the weaknesses of the classroom. Connected educators embracing voice need to be ready to receive the unfiltered feedback of kids. This can be uncomfortable. Student voice can enrich learning, but it comes with the daggers about the quality of each minute of instruction that teachers bring to the table. With the motto of "together with students," connected classrooms can pour student voice over the rich instruction already taking place and maximize engagement for all learners throughout the ecosystem.

THE CLASSROOM CONNECTION

Christine Ruder models the heart of being a connected teacher through her work with elementary students in mid-Missouri. Her story speaks deeply about the importance of giving students the opportunity to have voice. Christine has found classroom blogging to be an incredible opportunity to foster connected learning with her students. The story of Beau is one with which we can all deeply connect to, as it pushes us to reach more students with greater innovative ways of engagement.

Used with permission from Christine Ruder.

Connecting kids in one class with those in other classes is not a new phenomenon in education. We have been doing this for decades (even since I was a kid). We have done postcard projects (mail a postcard to another class in each state to learn about other states), Flat Stanley projects (send a Stanley replica to someone and follow his adventures through photos and a daily diary), and pen pals. The common denominator with all of these projects is a desire to have the kids make connections and to make learning more meaningful.

I am a huge believer in having kids blog for this reason. Not only does it provide an authentic purpose for writing, it can provide students with an authentic audience as well (instead of an audience of one . . . the teacher). I have been having my third graders blog for several years now. They love it because it uses technology, and they feel grown up writing on a blog. They also get excited about writing because they realize that their product is going on the Internet, and it can be read anywhere in the world . . . "even in China."

A couple years ago, I had a student from a very poor background. This family didn't have much. Beau hated to write. To be honest, he wasn't a big fan of school at all. We had been blogging in class once a week for about four months. One of my students, Susan, wrote a fantastic story and chose to share it on her blog. I wanted to ensure that more people saw her post so I tweeted the link out to share her work several times that day, using the #comments4kids hashtag. Several people commented on Susan's story. Most were teachers from the US, but she had one from Australia and one from New Zealand. This created quite a sense of excitement in our classroom the next day when Susan discovered that not only did she have comments, but comments from all over the world. We discussed commenting and reminded them how they can respond to their commenters, create a dialogue, and make a connection.

A few weeks later, I got a notification that one of my students had posted to their blog (I use Kidblog, and I have the posts and comments set to be moderated through me before they are posted to the Web). I about fell over when I realized who had posted to their blog. It was Beau. The kid who hated to write had written a short paragraph to share with the world. I was dumbfounded. This was not only a kid who hated to write, but I also knew that he didn't have a computer or Internet at home. I couldn't tweet the link fast enough to make sure that someone, anyone, would comment and reinforce Beau's efforts to write. The connections I made on Twitter responded wonderfully, and many people responded to Beau's post. When he came to school on Monday and logged in to his blog, he was so pleased to see that people not only saw his writing, but took the time to respond. He read each comment as if it were golden and responded to a few of them. He was so proud of himself. A few weeks later, he shocked me again by writing another post on his blog. Again, it wasn't much, but he was taking his free time to write and share.

It was another month before I found out the rest of the story. I was bragging about Beau to his mom and telling her how proud I was that he was taking the time to blog on his own time at home. When I asked mom about them getting a computer, she told me that they were thinking of getting one soon because she was going back to school to get her GED. I then turned to Beau and asked how he had blogged. Had he gone to the library? Had he been at a friend's house? No, he told me that he had used his Nintendo DS and his neighbor's Wi-Fi. I had to admire the kid for his ingenuity in making sure he could blog from home.

This kid had an audience. He had a purpose for writing for others. He made connections. He was feeling the power of voice. His writing improved over the rest of the year. He wrote more posts in class. He commented on others' blogs. Stories like Beau's remind me that writing, blogging, and other opportunities to give students voice and authentic audience are the two keys to an engaging, fun place to learn.

ACTION STEPS

1. ***Start a blog.** There is something about putting your written work into a public space that changes things. For teachers and teacher leaders this can be a risk, but the upside is a new vulnerability that has huge benefit for adult learners. Knowing how the blogging process works also creates a glide path for working through the logistics of student blogging.
2. **Start a student leadership council.** Each connected classroom needs a small group that can serve as a sounding board for new teacher ideas. This group should also have an opportunity to bring honest feedback to the teacher about previous lessons and the things that are and are not working in the area of instruction and classroom management.
3. **Comment on student blogs.** Helping other teachers with their blogging efforts by serving as their authentic audience will circle back tenfold when you reach out for teacher support for real-world projects in your classroom. It only takes a few minutes to find students who are looking for comments on their work. Start with the hashtag #comments4kids if you need a launching point.
4. ***Use art to practice conversation.** Projecting art onto the wall for close examination is a good way to practice having meaningful conversation in class. Google Art Project provides some great tools to look deeply at masterpieces from around the world. Students need practice in noticing and finding the words to build conversation.

RESOURCES

The intentionality of our learning design plays an important role in the fulfillment of the connected classroom. From the light, sound, and contents of the learning space to the words that fill the spaces with ideas and caring, each provides an essential piece of the puzzle. These links lead to incredible opportunities for teachers and schools to explore how to maximize learning spaces and bring student voice into the forefront.

The Third Teacher (http://thethirdteacherplus.com/)

The Importance of Classroom Blogging—Edutopia (http://www.edutopia.org/blog/blogging-in-21st-century-classroom-michelle-lampinen)

Roots of Empathy (http://www.rootsofempathy.org/)

CHAPTER 8

Student Voice Breeds Opportunities to Change the World

The empowerment of voice facilitate big shifts.

ESSENTIAL QUESTIONS

1. How can we encourage the confidence of students to speak up?
2. Why does it often take crisis or yelling to be heard above the inertia of education?
3. Does building an action-oriented mindset within students maximize classroom learning?
4. How can a democratic classroom give voice to invisible people?

THE THEORY

It is easy to talk about the beauty of democratic principles, but it is quite difficult to build the structures and culture in classrooms that allow students and facilitators of learning to practice the messy reality of democracy building. Many classrooms have students build the rules and procedures to begin the school year. This is a worthy activity, but one of the lessons to go with this activity is that democracy is fluid and today's norms may need to evolve. Classrooms need to continuously return to these rules and procedures, and allow students to have dialogue about how they should change based on what has been learned through observation, data, and feedback. Classroom meetings are often another way to bring student voice and democratic principles into the learning. Classroom meetings are opportunities to listen and grow, and they are opportunities to teach students to disagree without being disagreeable. In some classrooms, these are sustained throughout the year, but in many, the demands of time can squeeze these democracy practicing opportunities out of the instructional mix.

Beyond these 1.0 practices to celebrate student voice and bring democracy into the learning space, there is a set of practices that often pushes the adults who support learning into a more uncomfortable space, but it can bring classrooms and schools into a deeper connection with a democratic learning ecosystem. This includes having students participate in deciding the consequences for peers who have gone beyond the norms of the organization, allowing students to voice concerns about teachers with whom they are struggling to connect, and having student plan rites of passage, such as graduation or other ceremonies. These examples and others go beyond the structures and concepts of the National Schools of Character. They begin to grow classrooms into true democracy incubators where students craft their civil voice.

Connected classrooms are looking for ways to get beyond talking about democratic principles to a place where the voices of those being served are paramount to the voice of those in service. Students growing in this type of learning space begin to feel the power that comes from a democratic culture. They begin to see that they play an essential role in speaking up for those who don't have voice, and they recognize that they are essential to making their school the type of place of which they can be proud.

Part of the role of all teachers serving as facilitators of learning is to foster a confidence and interest in students to be the solutionists needed to tackle the big, hairy problems of our interconnected global ecosystem as seen in Figure 1. One of the keys to building these types of students is to fine tune their belief that their voice matters. Students who have been muted through poor instructional opportunities or a

FIGURE 1

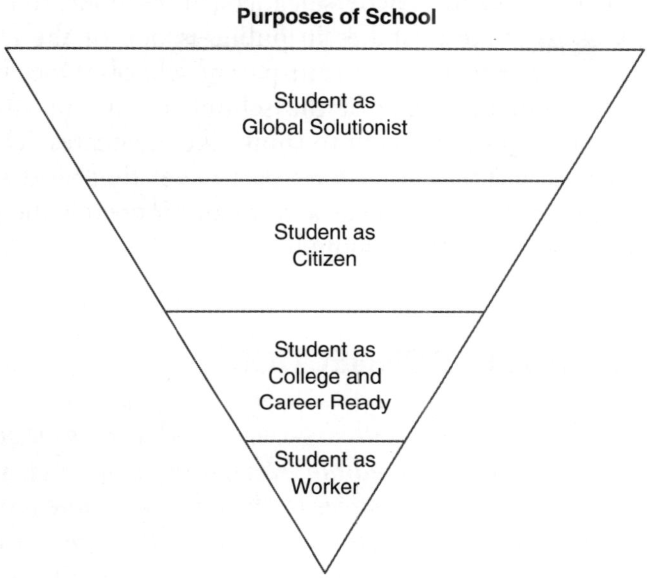

culture of compliance rarely are primed to step into the portion of their life beyond high school, where they are advocates for change. Instead, students are ready to "play school" and collect points.

The voice of students is powerful. It is often heard above the voices of adults when a stalemate around change has been reached. Imagine a school board meeting where the students come to the podium with well-thought-out ideas about how to change the athletic program to be more inclusive. They speak about how it could transform the school, and how they could rally the students to support the new ideas. The school board members in this scenario are leaning in and listening. In contrast, imagine a group of parents or the athletic director being at the heart of this new initiative. Who gets heard? Who breaks through the noise of the daily grind of school management? Clearly, the student voice has power.

With students, there is always learning to be had in this space. Students need to learn the tone and timing of bringing their voice into a professional space. They need to learn to be bold without being abrasive, and they need to learn clarity without being simple. In this space, it is easy for teachers, leaders, and schools to get jittery. Allowing kids to make mistakes in public is one of the leadership muscles that must grow in open, transparent schools. Once kids have their voice beyond the walls of the school, many amazing things begin to happen. Students begin to think like advocates. They begin seeing problems, and they can't look past issues that need attention. Empowering student voice breeds action, and it creates the platform for lifelong, passion-based learning.

THE CLASSROOM CONNECTION

Dave Steward leads a committed group of educators in southwest Missouri. He has shown incredible leadership at his high school to bring innovation and best practices to the table in a time when many other priorities could have dominated. Dave tells a story of coaching teachers in their connected learning journey. It is with nudges that Dave can grow the units of study in his high school classrooms. It takes connected leaders to support the courage of the connected educators who bring greater learning energy to the classrooms.

Used with permission from Dave Steward.

I always enjoy having conversations with teachers about how to take the next step with an instructional idea or project. One of my social studies teachers, Mr. Cook, and I recently talked about connected education. The conversation began with Mr. Cook having an idea to try a 20% time project in his sociology class. He indicated that one of the topics they cover in this semester course is current issues and their impact on society. Essentially, he wanted to allow the students to pick a social issue, research it, conduct surveys, and present their findings and recommendations. Any social issue of interest to the student was fair game. I was immediately in love with the idea because it allowed students to own the learning.

I followed up with Mr. Cook by posing a question. "How can we extend this to an audience beyond the school walls?" Mr. Cook's response was fairly typical. He thought that he should invite the superintendent and/or some school board members. Neither idea is bad, but I was looking for something beyond our community, something on a state or national scale. I asked him if he thought any topics might be political or legislative in nature. He indicated that they could be, but he was hesitant to ask legislators to come for a presentation or two because of their hectic schedules.

This is where the real transformation began to take place. I followed up with this question. “How can we leverage our technology to eliminate that concern?” I could see his excitement grow as we talked about the possibility of a virtual visit by a legislator or multiple legislators using Skype, Google Hangout, or FaceTime. He left and vowed to give it a shot. About a week later, I nudged him again by asking, “What do you want the impact of this project to be?” Mr. Cook indicated that he would like for his students to experience making an impact at the state or national level in some way.

This led to a discussion of setting high expectations for our students. I conveyed my belief that if he were to set the expectation that this project was designed to have an impact beyond our community, then his students would step up. They are the experts in teen social issues so they would own the project and work to make it have an impact larger than our town of Monett. Setting that expectation worked like a charm. Students produced some exceptional work around the topics of school lunches, laws regarding teens, and many other topics.

There was one presentation, however, that was beyond exceptional. One of the groups had done a study of bullying in the school and had found extremely surprising results. In fact, they used an audio presentation of a victim, with voice disguised, talking about her experience in the halls. Their presentation focused on the keywords she used and how we needed to work on solutions to bullying in our schools. This presentation was selected by our central office to be given as the board program at the next meeting of our board of education. Feedback from the board was positive, but we still wanted it to go farther.

After Mr. Cook and I talked, we wanted to get this presentation out to others, so he began to promote the project on Twitter. This led him to a few individuals from around the country who were interested in seeing the presentation. Some e-mails were exchanged and the feedback regarding the presentation was generally positive. While the project did not have the reach for which we had hoped, it was still a resounding success. Students from Monett High School produced a product that was reviewed by individuals who had never heard of the school. Our students realized that they could produce work that was worthy of review by someone outside of their classroom, their school, and their community.

ACTION STEPS

1. **Bring a student to the faculty meeting.** It is amazing how the behavior of adults shifts when students are present. They remain tuned into the essential topics of conversation, and they lean toward the students for answers. Having student voice in new places can be a catalyst for fresh insight and new angles for growth in a classroom and in schools.
2. **Shift the narrative:** Often it is said that history is written by the winners, and it is often through this lens that schools present their information. In a global world with varied cultural perspectives as a part of everyday work, it is essential for our students to hear and see the views of those who don't look like them. It means pushing through to other viewpoints that round out the conversation.
3. *****Say yes.** Empowering students means saying yes to student ideas. It means building a classroom culture that allows kids to believe that their voice will not only be heard, but it will be validated and supported. Saying yes to projects. Saying yes to easy requests. Saying yes to parallel learning. All these yes moments make it easier when no has to be the answer. It also paves the way for students to step up and practice taking action.
4. **Name the need to evolve.** Students often feel that the only chance that they get to contribute to the rules, norms, and culture is during the first day or two of school. Be sure to tell them in a connected classroom that everyone is a part of a growing ecosystem that needs adjustments and midcourse corrections. Be sure to schedule time to make these tweaks, based on student voice, throughout the year.

5. ***Seize their pain.** Students are vocal about the things that upset them. Sometimes they are just venting, but other times they notice issues in a way that no adult can. In these moments we have to seize their pain and begin to help them shape their voice so that it will be heard by a larger audience. Great connected educators bring together student concerns with the right audience to hear it.

RESOURCES

There are a variety of ways that the connected classrooms can promote the learning that excites students. Students who are allowed to create, make, and design during some part of their school day produce incredible work products, a hunger for more learning, and a desire to be heard beyond the wall of the school. Use these links to explore ways to begin to create these classrooms..

Center for Student Work (http://elschools.org/student-work)

20% Time—A Video (https://www.youtube.com/watch?v=KwwdtQHqd9g)

Stuvoice.org—A Community Dedicated to Student Voice (http://stuvoice.org/)

Responsive Classroom (https://www.responsiveclassroom.org/)

National Schools of Character (http://www.character.org/schools-of-character/national-schools-of-character-overview/)

Danez Smith on Student Voice (http://youtu.be/-v51H2R88VY)

CHAPTER 9

The Final Resting Place for Student Work

Excellent student work comes from producing for others.

ESSENTIAL QUESTIONS

1. How can we use authentic audience to expand the work of our students?
2. In what ways has the concept of thin classroom walls impacted the learning of your students?
3. What level of transparency around instruction is needed to attract meaningful partnerships for classrooms?

THE THEORY

By working to be open and transparent, courageous educators can begin to bring new life to their classrooms. The connected world allows this to occur at an ever-accelerating pace. Educators working to make this a reality in their classrooms are turning to audiences outside the four walls of their classrooms. They are turning to authentic audiences to provide feedback, support, and real-world energy to the hard work of the students. Doing this requires building a network of partnerships in the community and beyond with educators and noneducators whom the teachers and students can rely on to support the growth happening in the classroom. The best partners play a role in the entire learning process of a unit.

Authentic audience partners bring ideas for learning to the table. In this scenario, a business partner is looking for fresh ways to market their product to kids, and they would like student groups to use the same market research process as their professionals to get a unique look at an issue in which they are struggling for new perspective.

Authentic audience can also be used for feedback. As students work through an inquiry project about water, are they getting feedback from engineers? Are they using the design thinking process to grow their empathy about the user experience that the community has with water? Are they looking for models outside their community on which to base their solutions? All of these opportunities to learn from the ecosystem beyond the classroom provide students an additional push toward excellence.

This is the same for the growth of teachers as well. As teachers are transparent with their work through blogging, sharing, and reflecting with allies, they are pushing themselves to grow to new heights. As teachers are reaching out to those who excel in their niche of the profession, they are seeing new resources, bending their learning, and growing to new places.

For students, it is important to have authentic audience at different points of the learning. This includes during the first iteration of a project as well as in the final phase of study. Doing so allows greater excellence to grow around the students' work over time. Authentic audience makes the teacher less of the information expert and more an expert at surrounding students with innovative resources, ideas, and opportunities.

THE CLASSROOM CONNECTION

Rob Lamb teaches the importance of science to students in the Saint Louis area. Always looking for fresh ideas and a chance to make things real, Rob tells a story about being authentic, having authentic audience, and providing true authentic assessment. Rob provides some great concrete examples of how to bring a greater transparency to the learning that students experience.

Used with permission from Rob Lamb.

Authentic assessment is crucial in creating a classroom that has value beyond the school room door. Simply put, if you want to make students care about what they learn, it needs to engage them in a real way. The lessons that I remember from my childhood were the ones that meant something to me personally. When teachers create a lesson plan, they not only need to think about curriculum standards but also how the content relates to the student. One of the easiest ways to do this is by creating authentic assessments.

When creating authentic assessments, it is important not to fall into the pitfalls of giving a scenario such as, "OK class, today we are going to imagine we are writing an article to someone who works in a big oil company and explain to them why they are involved in bad environmental practices. In this letter you need to remember to tell the imaginary person how they have damaged the environment both in short- and long-term ways. Don't forget to write it in a five-paragraph essay."

- This is so close to being a high-quality authentic assessment. To take it to the next step, make the students find a real CEO of an oil company to write, and then have them research real problems the company has made for the environment. Finally, send the letters. The student will then feel the assignment has meaning and an audience beyond the classroom.

- When making assignments, the easiest way to make them authentic is to change the audience. By moving the audience from the teacher to anyone else, the lesson becomes more valuable. Students love to be heard, so let them. Take the assignment to the Web and let them share. Knowing that their thoughts will be heard by others makes students think a bit more about what they are saying.

- Here are just couple of examples from my class, showing how I have used authentic assessment:
  - **Read aloud/think aloud:** The number one way in which I have added connections to the content is by doing a read aloud/think aloud. A read aloud/think aloud is quick and easy. I pick an infographic or article on my subject, put it up on the projector screen, read it aloud, and describe my thinking. As I read, I give my reactions to the material, and walk through my thinking and where my mind wanders when reading the infographic. This allows students to see my thought processes, and I teach them how to think critically and look critically at data. This, in itself, is very powerful and personal. I am letting them into my mind. As a side note, this process creates a closer connection with my class because they begin to share how I look at this information.
  - **Wiki/blog:** I have a blog for students to post comments on both science articles and infographics. They comment on one another's comments also, and gain greater understanding by giving feedback to each other's questions. They also have to follow good digital citizenship practices to be responsible on the Internet.
  - **Production:** My chemistry students have a research project each semester in the form of an infographic. They must pick a topic within chemistry or biochemistry and find the data needed to create an infographic. Using a variety of tools, they create infographics on the subject they have chosen. They create several versions, which all receive journalistic-style edits, either from peers, professional editors, or me. To create an infographic, the student must understand the data on a far deeper and more personal level than they ever would for a research paper. As part of a grant, I have them submit the infographics to scijourner.org for possible publication. Some of them do get published either in print or digitally. In this project, the students

> know up front that I am not the audience. By changing the audience from me to their peers, they naturally step up the work. Also, by creating five to seven versions, they learn it isn't just a rough draft, final draft system. They also learn that just because they think it is finished does not mean it is finished to a level that is acceptable for publication.

When adding authentic assessments to your classroom, just remember the students want to bring meaning to their learning even if they don't know what that looks like or means. If you can't bring value to that information in a real way, then why are you teaching it in the first place?

ACTION STEPS

1. **How would you like to be assessed?** Teachers' honest answers to this question rarely is congruent with the way that teachers assess their students. It is so important to bring honesty and openness to the process for giving students' meaningful feedback. Thousands upon thousands of hours are lost giving poor feedback.
2. **Find ten people.** Chances are good that there are excellent teachers in your subject that would love to collaborate with someone of your quality. Stretch yourself to find ten excellent educators from around the country who can support your learning and teaching at a deep level. Develop curriculum together. Share resources and materials. Lean on their wisdom.
3. ***Try two new technology tools a quarter.** Commit to using two new technology tools each quarter that can bolster engagement in the classroom. These tools can amplify your teaching or support the learning opportunities that kids already have. Two is a realistic number, and it provides room for one of them to be a massive failure. Using new technology also creates new problems for you to solve and opportunities for you to explore.

4. **Look for adults to surround your kids.** Every child deserves another adult to surround them in learning, no matter if they already have 1 or 100. Knowing this creates an opportunity lens where all teachers are looking for creative ways to link the coalition of the willing to the needs of the individual students in their classrooms.

RESOURCES

Transparency is a hallmark of the new connected classroom. David Price's book *Open* is a true eye-opener around the speed and intensity in which education and classrooms need to progress in the area of deprivatization of practice. The other two resources below are tools students can use to to practice publishing their work to an authentic audience through a variety of online media.

Open by David Price (http://engagedlearning.co.uk/?page_id=40)

Communicating Through Infographics (http://www.easel.ly/)

The Learning Network—Great place for students to practice commenting on other students' work as well as publishing their own thoughts. (http://learning.blogs.nytimes.com/category/student-opinion/)

CHAPTER 10

Engaging Your Community as Listening Partners

Developing authentic audience requires a bench of meaningful partnerships.

ESSENTIAL QUESTIONS

1. With what networks of people do you communicate to grow your bench of active classrooms partners?
2. As a connected teacher, in what ways are you willing to sacrifice part of your time to support the work of one of your community partners?
3. How have you been successful in telling an interested partner that the synergy between their strengths and your classroom vision doesn't align?

THE THEORY

Friendships, helping hands, and partnerships are all very different ways for the community to connect with a classroom. Each is important, and each has its place. The best teachers find the right niche for everyone interested in playing a part of the students' learning in the classroom. Friends come for Grandparents' Day, the Valentine's Day parties, and the poetry slam. They show interest in the learning of the classroom by being present and showcasing to kids that adults care about their learning. They cheer. They clap, and they take pictures at the band and orchestra concerts. These friends in learning support the classroom beyond the school day, during the 18 hours when students aren't in school, by asking questions, purchasing supplies, and reminding the students about the importance of school. Friends of the classroom are so essentially important.

Helping hands go beyond friendship. They take an interest in a project, an idea, or the charisma of a teacher, and they begin to support classrooms with their time, talents, and treasures. Helping hands donate shovels for the service learning project, open their doors for students to visit their place of work, and make donations to a classroom that is doing work that they feel is excellent. This group of people brings support to classrooms in times of ever-shrinking resources, and they are essential inspiration for excellent teachers to attempt courageous things. Helping hands can also influence classes through donations to school foundations, contributing to capital campaigns, and giving to organizations such as Donors Choose.

Beyond these two groups, there are deep partnerships cultivated by classroom leaders and school leaders. Partnerships, unlike friendships and helping hands, are individuals and groups that are missional about joining students in their efforts to grow into productive citizens. This often means long-term commitments to classrooms in a variety of ways. Partners are willing to sacrifice part of their mission to amplify the work of the classroom. They are willing to work in concert with students on projects, pushing aside their age and wisdom to learn and grow with students. Great partners listen and accept that their work may never make the headlines or help in marketing their company. Classroom partners have a greater sense of community, and they know that their efforts will help grow their communities into more vibrant and sustainable places. Classrooms need these partners. They need deep sustainable relationships.

The process for developing these partners can be a messy one, as it takes time to reach out, grow, and evaluate whether there is the mutual connection that can last. Attempts to partner will fizzle out even with fantastic early energy, and other connections will emerge from almost nothing. Teachers need a keen sense of awareness and openness to make the most of the right opportunities for kids, as the benefits to having these partnerships are numerous, including mentorships, a sharing of learning duties, and fresh voices to push instruction into more meaningful places.

THE CLASSROOM CONNECTION

Jennifer Tiller has served students in the Saint Louis area in many capacities with the common link always being a quest for excellence. Her story speaks to partnerships and how schools no longer have the capacity to go it alone and get the results they need from kids. Jennifer talks about how she worked to build a village around the students she served so that they all had quality choices beyond high school.

Used with permission from Jennifer Tiller.

Harvard's 2011 release of the Pathways to Prosperity Report identified America's heightened attention to channeling students into a four-year college track only to have approximately half the nation's midtwenty-year-olds still ill-prepared for the workforce. A call to action was issued to create "innovation high schools" linking rigorous academics with work-based learning experiences to better prepare all students for both college and career.

Pattonville School District responded to that call by developing a plan called "Pattonville's Pathway to Success." While still in the early stages of implementation, it has developed short- and long-range plans to allow students the opportunity to access dual credit courses aligned to associate degrees, programs that result in industry-recognized credentials, and progressive work-based learning experiences. Bringing these opportunities to fruition has demanded curriculum articulation with postsecondary institutions, advisement from industry-specific committees, and collaboration with area businesses.

With support of grant monies awarded by the Missouri Department of Economic Development, Pattonville found its entry point in the high-demand career fields of advanced manufacturing, information technology, and health/medical professions. This led to the high school staff meeting with postsecondary staff to develop pathways, and offering dual credit that lead to degrees in computer-integrated manufacturing and information systems. Additional opportunities can lead to industry-recognized credentials in the information technology and health care fields. Using these pathways, students have the potential to leave high school with as many as 20 hours of articulated and dual credits.

Developing partnerships with area businesses has been critical to guide the opportunities created for students. Pattonville developed industry-specific advisory committees in each pathway to identify competencies, review curriculum, and clarify appropriate work-based learning experiences. With business input, they have developed a progressive continuum affording students the opportunity for a work-based learning experience each year at Pattonville High School. This begins with a professional speaker series, during freshman advisory, for students to learn more about careers within their chosen pathway of interest and aptitude. At the sophomore level, students may take a field trip day to participate in a job shadowing experience or elect to participate in a virtual job shadow. During their junior year, students may participate in industry or real-world challenges posed by businesses in their career pathway. At the senior level, students have the opportunity to participate in career internships both during and after the school day. While many of these experiences have been available to students in the past as self-directed or created experiences, staff members are now coordinating and promoting these learning opportunities.

Through Pattonville's advisory program, all staff members play a role in guiding students in their career choices. To support and promote staff learning of these connections, the district has worked with business partners to create externship experiences for the Pattonville staff. Additionally, vertical teaming with middle school guidance staff assures a smooth transition for students as the program creates system-wide career learning experiences and exposure before they enter the high school.

With innovation at the heart of this initiative, it is important to continually seek new learning opportunities for students and staff alike. The latest innovations include: the development of a help desk curriculum as students work in our IT service center to support one-to-one laptops, collaboration with postsecondary institutions to develop an onsite emergency medical training program, exploration of biotechnical curriculum connections, and participation in professional development institutes creating project-based learning units informed by business partners.

ACTION STEPS

1. ***Volunteer.** As teachers, we are always looking for volunteers for a variety of things, but have you experienced being a volunteer in a while? Knowing the user experience of being a volunteer will allow you to fine tune it for those opportunities surrounding your classroom. This tuning will help blossom your partnership bench.
2. **Let things run their course.** It is hard to say good-bye to partnerships and those who support classrooms, but there are moments when those who supported us are taking more energy than we are getting in return for the kids. We have to be willing to say that things have run their course or that the learning in your classroom has evolved to a place of needing a new partner.
3. **Beg, borrow, and steal.** Other people's partners may be right for you as well. Some partners may be looking to scale into additional schools. Some may have funds available to your school and not their other partners. Talk to other connected classrooms about the partners they have cultivated so you know the landscape and what's available.
4. **Grab low-hanging fruit.** There are plenty of opportunities for partnership. Often, classrooms are shooting for the moon when it comes to big corporate partnerships or grants. While this is wonderful when it happens, make sure to build some momentum around financial and in-kind support with smaller donations and gifts. There is much to learn in the development world, so practicing small may land the big fish.

RESOURCES

Surrounding a classroom with the right partners and support can be a daunting task for many. It isn't always natural for teachers to reach beyond their walls for the additional support for excellent learning to occur. Each of these links provides some paths to increasing the partnership capacity in the connected classroom.

Donors' Choose (http://www.donorschoose.org/)

Jobs for the Future—Pathways to Prosperity (http://www.jff.org/)

National Council for Community and Education Partnerships (http://www.edpartnerships.org/)

CHAPTER 11

The World as the Playground for Learning

Taking advantage of global connection expands classroom horizons.

ESSENTIAL QUESTIONS

1. What benefits come from students learning from other students in different countries?
2. Where in your curriculum could you make global connections?
3. How do technology tools allow students to create artifacts of learning that can be shared and used around the world?

THE THEORY

Students working in a digital environment have an increasingly broad range of opportunities to interact, grow, and share with authentic audiences globally. As students move through elementary school and into middle school, the need for context in learning grows. Students are looking for ways to connect both their formal and informal knowledge gained to this point in their academic careers. Recent advances in technology allow real-time collaboration including videoconferencing and instant document collaboration. These technology tools also take students beyond the abstract and allow students to take on simulated roles such as researchers, producers, and scientists.

Many students complain that their only class work is of the dull refrigerator door variety. They find it difficult to understand their place within a system without the opportunity to take on a realistic role. Teachers must take advantage of students' energy in this space by providing a growing global audience for their students. Unlike authentic audience in the community, stretching students into a global learning space also brings questions about culture, attitude, work ethic, and drive into the forefront for students to consider as they try to find their place in a global marketplace. As more and more students have these opportunities to be linked to authentic audiences and learning opportunities around the globe, teachers are seeing higher-quality work. Figure 2 illustrates how authentic audience impacts the quality of work.

Students are no longer looking to their classroom to be their primary space for receiving knowledge. They are using online spaces to drive their passion-based learning. Students are tapping into the collective wisdom of the crowd and becoming experts in a variety of fields.

FIGURE 2

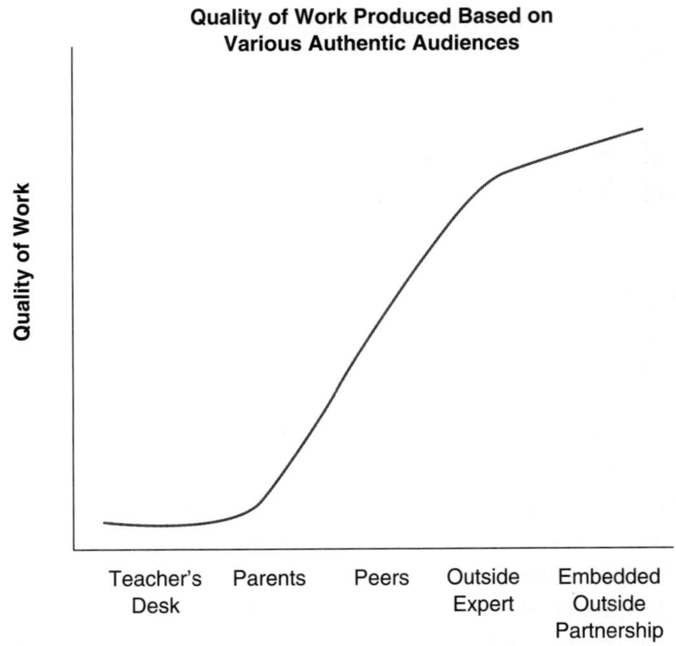

When students learn from a peer community of equals rather than a single authority, they contribute more, strive for excellence, and respond better to feedback. Schools desiring to remain relevant in this era of digital transformation must be nimble and see trends as learning opportunities. No longer will the final audience of the teacher in the front of the room draw the passion necessary for maximize engagement, but it will take a global audience to energize the learning of the connected classroom.

THE CLASSROOM CONNECTION

With a local mission and a global vision, William Chamberlain shares his questions and ideas about education with anyone who will listen. William lives in southwest Missouri, but is known throughout the state as the consummate connected educator. William's story about his students learning from students in the Middle East is a piece about what is possible. His courage to connect and push for even deeper learning gives his students experiences that would never have been positive just a decade ago.

Used with permission from William Chamberlain.

I often tell my students that they need to be intentional and not reactive. I truly believe that thinking things through can help us prepare to act appropriately and not worry about how we might react poorly. The funny thing is that the most important sequence of events for me that took place online happened because I reacted.

It all started in Qatar when Jabiz Raisdana decided to take his daughter Kaia outside and have her take pictures of what she saw in an empty lot. He tweeted a link that I happened to see. I planned to have my class leave comments on other students' posts that day, so I decided to have that post be one of them.

While the classes were commenting, Jabiz noticed the large number of comments coming in and sent another tweet asking whose students were leaving all the comments. I responded and let him know that my students had questions about where he lived. He suggested he could Skype us, and we immediately agreed. My students asked Jabiz many questions about Qatar, and I remember vividly seeing their faces as he explained how wealthy the country is and how well developed. Their misconceptions of Middle East countries had exploded, leaving them with a real sense of uncertainty. Later, I showed them pictures of Qatar's cities, and they were amazed.

Jabiz explained to the class that Kaia wasn't old enough to read yet, and he suggested that they may want to make some video comments. I decided to connect them through Voicethread. I quickly wrote a short narrative of the events that happened, took a few screen shots, and created the Voicethread that I then shared with Jabiz.

The story didn't stop there. Dr. Strange, a professor at the University of South Alabama, saw the events take place and had his students create comments for Kaia as well. They went on to have Jabiz Skype their class and create videos back and forth with Kaia. This series of events convinced Dr. Strange to require his students to comment on student posts as part of his class; since this happened, his students have left thousands of posts on students' blogs.

This series of events affected me. I now know the power of the Internet, especially how blogging has the ability to connect people in powerful and meaningful ways. I have seen others take this story and share it with people all over the world. The power of the story comes not from the tools we used to create it, but from the sharing of our experiences with one another. Since then, I have been involved in many other events where connections have been made through blogging. I have seen friendships develop—painful and joyous events have been shared between connected friends. My personal and professional life has been enriched by these stories, and I hope the same for my students as well.

ACTION STEPS

1. ***Look for some potentially easy connections.** Do you know someone living overseas? Are you connected to any educators who serve students in a different country? Do any of your students have connections to a foreign country? Is there a military base, international school, or corporation in your town with connections in a foreign country? Try connecting your classroom through one of these avenues.

2. **Think about creating an authentic audience on a global scale.** It is often easy to make connections to social studies units and a variety of literature topics, but in math and science, the connection isn't always as obvious. Look for issues of scarcity to make connections in science as well as issues surrounding systems and systems thinking. In math, think about projects and programs involving statistics, engineering design, and information literacy. All of these are emerging fields in math in which every country on the planet is looking for answers.
3. **Who will respond?** It is amazing for kids to know that their questions are valued by folks around the world. Students can get personal responses from foreign leaders, scientists, and other area experts. They can elicit comments about their work from others, and collaborate on citizen science and data collection projects that are happening in real time.
4. **Celebrate your responses and partners in learning.** The key, as always, is to pick a space, take a risk, and allow learning to happen differently. Students will be eager to make these connections. It will ramp up their engagement, and it will provide fresh opportunities for deep connections and empathy building in the interconnected global economy in which all students are connected.

RESOURCES

This set of links revolves around the incredible journey of William Chamberlain's connected classroom that was looking to grow deeply around the understanding of a culture and place around the world. This class was able to use blogging, commenting, and the power of video to unlock learning that would have been unavailable just a few years ago. Follow this journey from its primary sources.

Connected Student/Parent Blog Examples (http://www.jabizraisdana.com/blog/singing-hearts/) (http://dearkaia.blogspot.com/2009/09/first-photo-essay.html)

Will Chamberlain's Journey With Blogging and Connecting (http://mrcsclassblog.blogspot.com/)

Story About the Power of Global Connection (http://edm310fa112009.blogspot.com/2009/11/kaia-reads-book-and-her-father-skypes.html)

CHAPTER 12

Authentic Audience Grows Innovative Learners

Growing student capacity around a digital footprint amplifies with authentic audience.

ESSENTIAL QUESTIONS

1. How does building a connected classroom impact our duty to grow digital citizens?
2. How do the strengths of students play a role in crafting their digital footprint?
3. Why should students be building their "brand" by design?

THE THEORY

Someday digital citizenship will just be known as citizenship just like cyberbullying will be known as bullying and 21st-century learning will be known as learning, but until then, it is essential that classrooms embed the skills of being civil in online spaces as part of the portfolio of learning that takes place. The way students handle themselves in social spaces is awkward, and the way they handle themselves in social online spaces can be downright confusing. Connected students are working on identity in an open, transparent way that is vulnerable and raw. It is messy and confusing for them and even more so to the people who surround them. They are sorting out how to behave, be accepted, and be themselves.

In these spaces, there are mistakes, a lack of common sense, and, in a few cases, mistakes that have disastrous long-term impacts.

In a time when the best classrooms are inviting risk taking and failing forward with student work, there remains a struggle to parlay those invitations for risk taking and failing forward into the digital realm. Many classrooms are still looking to avoid digital mistakes as opposed to help students grow through digital errors. Schools are finding ways to punish and filter as opposed to teach, reteach, and build the conditions for success.

Most students have a digital footprint. They have filled it with photos, tweets, and comments, but in the best classrooms, students are given opportunities to be intentional about their digital footprint. These students are building a positive personal brand that will guide, shape, and limit the poor choices around digital footprint. To do this, students are working from their strengths. They are writing songs, creating art, writing books, and making useful household items. They then place this work in the global marketplace for feedback. They ask buyers from throughout the world about whether they have a product that has market value. They learn about cost, discounts, and marketing, and they begin to see the potential of entrepreneurship.

During this process, students are learning that negative words, images, and activities related to them can impact their ability to grow their brand and grow a customer base. Embedded in these opportunities are other lessons about digital behavior. Students are given opportunities to interact with other websites that are successful based on feedback loops created by users including online book reviews, online stores, and digital reviews of services that are available in the community.

Students in classrooms dedicated to growing civilians are learning about the digital marketplace and how it functions. Case studies surround these connected classrooms as they examine the pitfalls others have made in damaging their digital image and footprint. Students in deeper learning surrounding these topics become an active part of the solution in digital spaces. They are using their rights as citizens to be heard, to explain, and to persuade. They are learning what to do as digital citizens and not just what to avoid. Knowing that life is an authentic audience is a key to growing the local and global citizens we need.

THE CLASSROOM CONNECTION

Chris McGee is an engine for education. His energy for kids, learning, and all that is right for education has helped teachers, leaders, and families in Saint Louis and around the country. His story highlights the power of choice and the importance of tapping into the passion for learning that is hardwired into all kids. Chris gives credit for his inspiration to the many members of his connected family, and he explains how taking a chance with time and resources paid huge dividends to the growth of his kids and the growth of the community.

Used with permission from Chris McGee.

What motivates kids? Why do kids do what they do? Why do they learn what they want to learn and not what I want them to learn? These questions, in addition to many others, sent me on a mission to learn more about motivation. My quest sent me to many different websites, books, resources, and people until I found two experts that forever changed my thinking about what my classroom could be. The first person I stumbled across was a fellow middle school teacher from Naperville, Illinois. Josh Stumpenhorst was active on Twitter (@stumpteacher), and he and I ran into one another through various conversations and chats. He was involved in an event called Innovation Day.

Josh energizes his classroom by putting the interests, passions, and talents of his students at the forefront. Innovation Day gives students a chance to investigate an idea and create something. Josh never fully knows what will come from each Innovation Day, but he provides structure and support so all students succeed. This sent me down a path that was truly uncomfortable, risky, and exciting. Needless to say, he rocked my world.

The second person who had an impact on my study of motivation was Dan Pink (@danielpink), the New York Times bestselling author. I watched his TED talk, and marveled about the simple concepts that are the hidden keys of motivation. These keys are mastery, autonomy, and purpose.

Allowing students to work toward mastery at their own pace engages and motivates them to accomplish a task. Autonomy allows students to choose their path by infusing personalization and choice into their learning. The final attribute is purpose. Purpose has students working toward clear and concise learning goals, often with authentic audience, so they know what is expected of them.

Innovation Day also led me down the path of infusing the concept of 20% time into my classroom. This project may not be directly tied to curriculum. Accomplishing this was not an easy task. First, it means whittling down the curriculum to get to the core concepts, and then getting kids to master these core concepts just to create the space and time to attempt it.

"I want you to do something. I don't care what it is, I just want you to investigate, take apart, create, make, build, and learn about something." Granted, the first projects were pretty hit-or-miss, but they quickly went from good to amazing. The sharing day was always my favorite. It was a great way to celebrate learning and the idea of getting better at a task or concept.

Student motivation and engagement are tricky subjects, but giving up control and power, shifting to mastery, autonomy, and purpose, and providing authentic audience yields powerful learning. You will see kids being excited about learning something new, creating something with their hands, and investigating why something happens the way it does. I went into teaching to inspire students, and 20% time reenergized and refocused me on making my students the core of the classroom.

ACTION STEPS

1. ***Plan your 20% time.** Too many teachers love the idea of 20% for their students, but they don't think about their 20% time. What would you do if you had 20% of your time to create? Could one plan period a week be used for you to work on a project that isn't related to your job? Feeling the power of 20% only increases the interest in bringing it to the classroom.

2. **Start an online marketplace.** Students need to learn to navigate the digital marketplace. This includes learning how to leave reviews on sites such as Amazon, AirBnB, and Uber. It means knowing about Square and PayPal and learning how to take pictures and write descriptions for the places that sell our goods.
3. *****Be a Kiva classroom.** Kiva.org is a microlending organization that provides individuals, groups, and classrooms the opportunity to contribute loans to those with needs around the world. Being a global citizen and being a digital citizen overlap. Knowing this and experiencing this are essential pieces of growth in the connected classroom.
4. **Spend time reflecting on adult digital mistakes.** There are certainly plenty to choose from in the media. Real meaningful conversation around these high-profile cases can help students navigate the waters. Discussing the long-term impact of these mistakes also squeezes the celebrity status out of the choices.
5. *****Take an online course.** The organized online learning options have been chaotic over the past years, but it is beginning to find its stride regarding quality and content. Being able to navigate online learning platforms from sign-up, to collaboration strategies, to ways to remain engaged throughout the course are all skills that teachers must courageously wade into to support the future growth of the kids in their classrooms who will be learning in those places.

RESOURCES

Being a digital citizen is clearly becoming another part of being a quality citizen in the global marketplace of ideas. The key for the connected classroom, which uses authentic audiences as part of its work, is to make digital citizenship a daily, embedded part of the work. These links can support a teacher in crafting the right set of expectations and activities for their innovative connected classroom.

Dan Pink on Motivation (http://www.ted.com/talks/dan_pink_on_motivation)

Josh Stumpenhorst's Blog on Innovation Day (http://stumpteacher.blogspot.com/search?q=innovation)

Digital Citizenship Scope and Sequence (https://www.commonsensemedia.org/educators/scope-and-sequence)

Your Digital Dad—Kevin Honeycutt's Series on Digital Footprint and More (http://www.youtube.com/playlist?list=PLLyzas11KuPpmLgJSKWI_QpmeUAgBNATe)

Lulu.com—A Place to Self-Publish Kid's Thoughts (http://www.lulu.com/)

Etsy.com—A Place for Kids to Sell Their Creations (https://www.etsy.com/)

CHAPTER 13

When Communities See Students as Assets

Many communities see kids as liabilities; connected educators can change that.

ESSENTIAL QUESTIONS

1. What misconceptions does your community have about your classroom?
2. How can schools promote a healthy balance surrounding community involvement?
3. Which students have been the greatest assets to your classroom and/or community?
4. What mental models in your community are inhibiting innovation?

THE THEORY

Communities can be places that judge our kids for their individuality. They can be places that cause our students to be unsafe. Our communities can be filled with pessimism that sucks the energy out of the educational system. Our communities can struggle to see the potential of our students. The community—the loom that supports the learning pattern—can often unintentionally tangle the threads that educators are attempting to weave.

Not all communities are toxic in nature. Some are very neutral. They allow schools to do their work without interference. They work in parallel with the school, and they support the schools on a limited basis. It is only in rare times of crisis that these communities show energy to ask about what is occurring. It is a passive acceptance of how schools conduct their business. In these communities, there is often affluence or indifference. Each gives space even when space isn't a part of the solution.

Other communities are very involved. Parents and community members are actively questioning the school. Schools feel as though they are under scrutiny, and the pressure becomes a crucible. Parents and community members are often applying their own mental models of schools to their concerns about the current situation. Innovation and best practices are often minimized in these spaces as the community begs for tradition, comfort, and consistency to the past.

In contrast to all of these, most communities that surround the students who learn in schools have a much healthier presence. They see the school as a key asset, and they believe that much of the future health of the community will be based on the schools that reside within them. They support the schools by volunteering, and they reinforce the norms of the school. Healthy communities are opening their eyes to how schools have changed, and they are asking questions about what the changes mean. Healthy communities know that educating children is complex, and it can't be summed up or boiled down to a list. They accept that schools aren't the same as when they walked the halls, and the statement of solution, "You know in my day, we would have . . ." never is uttered.

The biggest difference between these healthy communities and toxic communities is their overall perception of students. In toxic communities, students are often seen as liabilities. They are seen as the kids who crowd into the restaurants only to order water and eat chips and salsa. They are seen as the kids who cause traffic jams by their poor driving and their walking in the streets. They are seen as the kids who are swearing in the park while a family tries to enjoy the sunset. Unhealthy communities grab the headlines about a single incident that includes students and generalize it to a much greater audience.

In healthier spaces, kids are viewed much differently. They are seen as hope. They are seen as future leaders. The healthy community understands that kids make mistakes and that one kid's poor choices aren't an indictment of all students throughout the community. The best communities are leaning in for the ideas of kids as they know that they come to issues with a fresh lens and a passion for solutions. They breathe in their desire to be change makers, and they embrace the reality that every student is learning from the community, so it is essential for the best parts of the community to step forward and play this key role.

Connected leaders can serve as a catalyst to shift communities. Having open classrooms and transparency around the learning that is taking place along with using the community as a classroom all begin to foster momentum in the favor of kids and, ultimately, in favor of the homes and neighborhoods that fill the communities.

THE CLASSROOM CONNECTION

Kevin Grawer is the principal of Maplewood Richmond Heights High School. He is a strong proponent of creating an academic culture built on positive relationships and a work-like atmosphere. Always promoting a positive growth mindset, Kevin says it's important to love your students and coworkers—meaning you have a "genuine concern for their well-being and have their best interest at heart." "Schools make an incredible difference in the lives of more people than any other institution, and we can't waste a day," states Kevin. An advocate for a sense of "calm urgency," Kevin takes pride in the academically rigorous culture that exists at MRH High School.

Used with permission from Kevin Grawer.

Renee was master teacher, and she didn't even know how good she was. It took a lot of coaxing from me to get Renee to finally admit that even with no formal training or sense of what was supposed to happen in the classroom, she could get kids to do amazing things. Renee oversaw our education for sustainability work. Her background was teaching adults how to grow backyard crops, be guerilla farmers, and permaculture—things that never showed up in any of our state standards.

She became interested in our school because she felt that it had the potential to be a leader in teaching and learning about sustainability. She had a vision about how sweet potatoes would make ground cover around the front of the garden, how an herb spiral could work with a new water feature, and how to produce berries and apples. She found soil that was perfect for peanuts, and she was excited because peanuts were native to Missouri and could be tied to the incredible story of George Washington Carver. Renee joined us in the summer during the peak of the growing season, and even with no kids to support her that first summer, she dirtied her fingernails, lost a lot of sweat, and showcased her dedication to the soil and the magic it can produce.

In the fall, when the students returned, I knew she would have her sink-or-swim moment. Even with the support of the fellow teachers and her administrators, it was hard to imagine her having incredible initial success with the kids, outside in the garden, without having the tricks of a skilled teacher. I was wrong, though. Renee was wildly successful. The kids jumped through the most ridiculous hoops for her. They harvested. They planted. They prepared. The garden was across from the public library, and the daily patrons started to take notice.

Renee worked hard during her time with the kids in the garden. I started to notice that more and more people were walking by and slowing down as they drove by to see the garden. I'd imagine that the students working in the garden had probably been yelled at by many of those neighbors to "get off our lawn" or "stop cutting through our backyard," but the garden and Renee's hard work began to reshape the perception of the community about our kids.

Renee came to me asking to have the students participate in the community farmers' market. She thought it would be great for them to know that their work in the garden could produce some money for the school. A group of students took turns running the table on Wednesday night. Almost every week, they would sell all of their items. Renee stood back as the students interacted with the adults at the farmers' market. She enjoyed watching the students demonstrate good customer service as well as seeing the reaction that many of the adults had.

About three weeks after the market opened, an older couple pulled me aside and told me that the student at the table lived behind them. They were used to seeing the student sitting out in the backyard by himself, but they had never talked to him until tonight. The couple said that they were going to help him build his own garden, but in their yard, so that he could escape to their space when he wanted.

When I shared that story with Renee, she felt that her hard work was coming to fruition. She knew that her garden, the farmers' market, and the loving community were helping to reshape the life of at least this student, but we were both certain that the number was much higher.

ACTION STEPS

1. **Attend a community meeting.** It is easy to get caught in the echo chamber of education, especially if we are actively learning online. It is important for teachers to find community places to listen. Some "community" meetings take place in the donut shop each morning, but others look like a planning and zoning city meeting. Connected educators must feel the pulse of the community to be wildly successful.
2. **Tell one. Tell one hundred.** Do you know the parents who serve this role? As a classroom teacher or teacher leader, it is important to know the parents who can spread the message of your classroom. It is important to feed these individuals with all of the good stuff.
3. *****Be visible in the community.** Once a month, go shopping in the community where you support learning. Stop for the local car wash even when your car is spotless. Order takeout on the way home from a place that you know is owned by a family in the school. Make time to see students in the community, no matter if that is showing cattle, a dance recital, or a karate belt ceremony.
4. **Talk about the complexity of learning and school.** The mental models that most communities have surrounding schools, at their core, are based on the memories of their personal experiences

with schooling. The complexity of learning and building the whole and connected child is so hard for most to grasp. Teachers must be champions of the complexity while telling a simple, compelling narrative.

RESOURCES

These resources support the idea that students are an essential part of the larger community. The conversations that these resources enrich include growing student awareness for the environmental needs of a community, putting students in the shoes of the adults that support the community, and thinking about ways that communities and schools can simultaneously support the development of a variety of student traits.

Communities in Schools (http://www.communitiesinschools.org/)

Schools and Community Gardens (http://www.gatewaygreening.org/)

Building Vibrant Communities (http://startempathy.org/about/changemaker-schools)

Search Institute's 40 Developmental Assets (http://www.search-institute.org/content/40-developmental-assets-adolescents-ages-12–18)

CHAPTER 14

Schools as Idea Incubators

Using processes like design thinking, students can develop valuable solutions for communities.

ESSENTIAL QUESTIONS

1. What benefits emerge from teachers growing as designers?
2. How can classrooms embrace design thinking for social change?
3. What does failing forward look like in your teaching life?

THE THEORY

Students as designers and students as solution-makers aren't the typical way most children in schools are described, but many connected classrooms are trying to change that because both are essential traits for our next generation of leaders. To build these traits, many classrooms are turning to the tools of design thinking that have emerged from the Hasso Plattner Institute of Design or d.school at Stanford University. At the heart of this work is building design, encompassing ideas such as: show don't tell, focus on human values, craft clarity, embrace experimentation, be mindful of process, mindsets, a bias toward action, and radical collaboration.

These concepts can take years to unpack and teach and decades to master, but they are the skills that are desired in the global marketplace.

With a foundation in these mindsets, connected classrooms are using design thinking to grow the solution-making DNA of students. Only through a deep understanding and knowledge of the user can meaningful change occur. This pushes students into an uncomfortable place as additional layers of ecocentrism are washed from their hearts, and the flood of social responsibility that comes from empathy building emerges.

Once empathy capacity begins to grow, classrooms are able to support students to not only see the obvious problems that need to be designed for, but to be true problem finders who dig to the heart of issues. These big, hairy problems are the ones that require the most study and observation, and they are also the ones that produce the most satisfaction when a locally designed solution emerges. In this process, students also have an opportunity to ideate, which blows up the conventional wisdom surrounding brainstorming and pushes young solution-makers to search deeply for ways to make change. Ideation is about generating fresh ideas and pushing thinking to a place beyond where the true solution lies.

So as connected classrooms use design thinking for learning, gems emerge including new mindsets, empathy building, problem finding, and creative solution making. The final lessons that come from using design thinking involve the lessons that emerge from prototyping and testing the solutions that are crafted. In this space, failing is expected and learning from feedback is a must. The concept of rapid prototyping showcases a way for students to explore potential solutions, reinfuse empathy through additional user feedback, and build better solutions through each iteration. Teachers are seeing the benefits of having design thinking as a core tenant to the learning of their connected classroom, as it allows students to contribute deeply to the solution making in schools and throughout the community.

THE CLASSROOM CONNECTION

Patrick Dempsey is an eighth-grade science teacher in the Webster Groves School District in the Saint Louis suburban area. He earned his master's in educational technology in 2010, became a Google Certified Teacher in 2013, and earned a second master's in educational administration in 2014. Patrick continues to grow in his understanding about fun and innovative ways to cultivate learning for his students. Patrick has a variety of experiences with Bring Your Own Device (BYOD), robotics, mobile learning, 1:1, flipped teaching, makerspaces, project-based learning, and standards-based grading. Patrick works to better the profession by facilitating professional development in a variety of districts and at conferences across the state.

Used with permission from Patrick Dempsey.

"I made it," said an eighth-grade girl in my science class who had just put the finishing touches on her cardboard miniature bowling game where fingernail polish bottles served as pins. It wasn't just any bowling game. It was a bowling game where upon knocking over a "pin," a Christmas tree light loosely poking out of cardboard at the top of the game turned on. It lit up because on the back of each fingernail polish bottle, there was aluminum foil that completed part of a circuit, turning on one light.

"I made it" is a proud statement. In three short words, you learn a lot about the person, the process, and the product. You know that the person has interest. You know that the process included failing, thought, and grit, and required more than one skill. You know that the product is unique to the maker, and it wasn't simply purchased or consumed. Consuming stops thinking, while making requires it. The bottom line is that students need to make, and my intensity around this statement has grown after letting my students loose on a project in our electricity unit where they had to make an arcade game out of cardboard that showcased their understanding of circuits.

When I told my curriculum coordinator and longtime partner in awesomeness about the project, he grew the idea (note: surround yourself with people smarter than you who build on ideas) by saying, "Yes . . . and you should take your games to an elementary school and invite kids to come and play." It was a masterful add-on that motivated students and celebrated their ingenuity. When students found out they were designing, making, and building for actual kids, they stepped up their game (pun intended). Our play day at a neighboring elementary school was a huge success. All I could do when looking around the gymnasium that day—at the real-world skills and teenage compassion in action—was gaze in awe. Upon reflection, one student wrote, "I didn't know my game was cool until a first grader got in line seven times to play it." Hold the phone people! A first grader validated the work of a too-cool-for-school eighth grader. Yes, that happened!

Any grade that I would have given a student on their project after that experience would have seemed cheap and contrived because audience has even greater value. Having teachers be the only ones who ever see the brilliance of student work is quite limiting. In a day and age where I can flip on a video chat and students can explain their homemade water filters to the CEO and founder of a not-for-profit company that is engineering water filters for third-world countries, why shouldn't student work have an audience? If I can't find an audience who would be interested in the work students are doing, then the students are doing the wrong kind of work.

Learning happened because I got out of the way of student thinking and, instead, became an expert on tools and resources and a guide in problem solving. It all started with a risk that I took because my students are worth it. Every student activity after this one seemed like factory work, and it had to be revised. Since this project, I have used the network of amazing teachers that I am connected with in person and on social networks to incorporate making an audience for student work.

ACTION STEPS

1. ***Make often.** Use your classroom as a space to make small-scale stuff with lots of low-cost materials. Cardboard, felt, and construction paper along with markers, glue, and Popsicle sticks should be in every classroom. Kids can flesh out their ideas with small prototypes. They can shift the learning in their head to their hands and back again.
2. **Think in solutions and notice problems.** As connected teachers, it is important to model solution making. Think through situations aloud, and ask students for fresh ideas and solutions often. In addition,

notice problems, mostly the little problems. Teachers who see the small problems around them help students notice things before others, a trait of successful designers.

3. **Add more writing surfaces.** Students need visible surfaces to showcase their ideas. It is easier than ever to make the walls, desks, or any smooth surface a place for ideas to blossom. Students get the vibe that ideas are important and that good ideas need to be left to marinate overnight. Multiple classes can work on surfaces together, and every moment of every day is a gallery walk.
4. ***__Make empathy building your bullying prevention strategy.__** At the core of being a designer is having empathy for those who will use the process, product, concept, or idea that is being designed. Connected classrooms are bringing this idea to the forefront, giving kids tons of time to practice empathy building and to hear the stories of others. The positive unintended consequence of empathy building is inevitably fewer kids treating each other poorly in the classroom and beyond.

RESOURCES

Classrooms that create, make, and design are seeing incredible learning emerge. For the teachers in the connected classroom, the key is weaving together this creation space with the core content. This is a tricky dance, but these links provide some great places to start and explore as teachers design unique learning experiences for kids.

Teachers as Designers (http://tedxtalks.ted.com/video/Teachers-as-designers-Annette-D)

The Stanford d.school Blog (http://dschool.stanford.edu/fellowships/)

Ideapaint (one solution for writeable walls) (http://www.ideapaint.com/)

Design Thinking for Educators (http://www.designthinkingforeducators.com/)

RESOURCES

CHAPTER 15

Service Learning

A Catalyst for Community Change

Student engagement is maximized through the core principles of service.

ESSENTIAL QUESTIONS

1. What do you see as the biggest challenges on the planet?
2. How does your classroom support the solution makers and problem identifiers who aren't great students?
3. How do you wrap learning around service?
4. What academic benefits come from injecting an ethic of service into classroom learning?

THE THEORY

With our hands in the dirt, there is a connection to nature and our creator, and with our hands stretched out in service to others, the view into our own souls grows in clarity. Serving and supporting the work and lives of others are essential threads in the social fabric of all classrooms, communities, and countries. Weaving an understanding about service into the time and space of learning can be a tricky proposition.

Our teachers who are connected beyond the walls of the classroom are finding the joy, beauty, and benefit from engaging in service and the learning that can be wrapped around it. In many places, service learning falls short of being meaningful service. This can create a garbled message about the potential of service for both students and the community. Communities are often gracious enough to allow students to tinker around doing things for the communities but struggle to support service that can make a substantial impact over time. This is because it requires a need for more planning, more synergy, and a greater willingness to partner with classrooms and work side by side with students. Connected classrooms are thoughtful about how the layers of service can be built over time, as seen in Figure 3.

Service without reflection is a gift, but service with reflection and the subsequent learning that comes that reflection creates the conditions necessary for building an ethic of service in the next generation of active citizens. It is this type of lofty vision that has teachers bringing

FIGURE 3

Building a K–12 Ethic of Service

kids to parks, nursing homes, and community centers. It is this same lofty vision that has students being uncomfortable and out of their element, going home exhausted from a long day of work, and celebrating the blisters on their hands.

Big challenges are in our future. As a planet, we will need a plan to feed more than nine billion people and to quench the growing need for water for consumption, agriculture, and industry. Another great challenge lies in transitioning our energy to a greater portfolio of renewable energy. These are massive undertakings and pose some of the greatest challenges of our time. The brightest minds work to build scalable solutions each day. Eventually, the minds charged with the work to enhance our planet will be coming from the classrooms of today. Those minds could include the quiet girl in the corner who is always reading a book or the noisy girl with pink hair and tons of opinions.

The next generation of solution makers won't come from those who take tests well, but those who learn, unlearn, and learn with artful agility. They will come from the students who think big and act often with no fear of failure. The future solution makers will come from classrooms that cultivate those skills. Cultivating the skills needed to lean into the biggest problems we face requires a classroom willing to take on big challenges and classrooms willing to pause some pieces of normal instruction to allow for the sparked passion of students to drive the learning.

This can happen as students hear about communities in distress from natural disasters such as floods, tornados, and earthquakes and then choose to rally for those in need. It can happen as students notice a local problem that inhibits the beauty of a community, and the class works to clean up a local watershed. It can be a desire by the class to raise awareness about cancer because one of their classmates is impacted. The students in classrooms willing to take on these challenges have a chance to feel the pleasure of serving, and they can feel the potential impact they can make as students. These are the feelings that continue as adults and allow us to truly fulfill the civil life that is an inherent duty of each citizen of this democracy.

To make this a reality, the acts of service must have impact and significance for the students. They must push students to see things differently and push down the selfish traits that simmer in the hearts of most students. Service learning allows for organic learning as well. When students have an opportunity to learn from adults who aren't a part of the daily classroom, fresh words spark fresh connections. Students working and sweating in service experience a humility that can provide perspective concerning the gifts with which they are blessed.

The world needs social entrepreneurs. It needs change makers. Both of these come from consistent practice in serving others. Embedding the ethic of service into the classroom allows the service to build on the subjects, topics, and units students and teachers are already experiencing together during the learning process.

It is the small actions that have big purpose in the world, and the students in the desks, classrooms, and schools throughout every community in the country deserve to know that they have the power to be the catalyst for awesome, mind-blowing change. There will be opportunities in each of their lives that, when seized, transform humanity in real and powerful ways.

THE CLASSROOM CONNECTION

Steve Himes, teacher and thought leader in Kansas City and beyond, shares his experience about the impact of service on his students. Steve has seen the girls at his school break through a lens of privilege to have a lens of social justice. He has enjoyed watching this evolution in his students from feeling nervous in service to developing a need to serve beyond their school. Steve shares with vigor that serving with grace is essential to a true education.

Used with permission from Steve Himes.

I teach at a Catholic, all-girls, college-prep academy in Kansas City that requires 60 hours of community service to graduate. Being affiliated with the church, the school has access to plenty of service opportunities throughout the city, but few students perform their service in the high-poverty parts of the urban core, even though it is a closer drive than many of the children's hospitals in the suburbs.

For the past few service weeks, I volunteered to observe a small group of girls who chose to volunteer at a small charter high school east of Kansas City's stark racial dividing line, Troost Avenue. Last year, the girls tutored a group of at-risk students for the state exam in English Language Arts, a large part of which is a five-paragraph essay. They told me that, at first, they weren't sure how to approach the students because they knew how to write the essay, but weren't sure how to teach it.

They decided to model their approach based on our peer-editing structure from sophomore English. I had created a critical analysis checklist of necessary writing skills, which students would use to evaluate each other's essays. Rather than immediately take the student's writing and tell them what's wrong, they invited the students to use the outline to evaluate examples of the *tutor's* writing. This gave the students the sense that this was a learning team and earned trust. At this point, the students got the idea, and tutors helped them evaluate their own writing as well.

As teachers, our goal is to not have them need us anymore. We know they don't need us when we can see them apply what they've learned without us assigning, guiding, and assessing them like the tutoring during service week. This is the paradox of education, especially public education: It's state-sponsored independence. Applied to our desire for authentic experiences, how do we make kids be entrepreneurial when, by definition, entrepreneurialism is a risk-taking venture out in the real world? These experiences have to happen outside school, unsupervised by teachers, but with teachers communicating with the supervising adults to provide accountability. This takes work, but community service projects are one way to do that.

A few public schools mandate service, as does the A+ Program in Missouri, but most of the time community service is unfeasible because kids are tied up with extracurricular activities and jobs. What we've done is set aside a week for juniors and seniors to do their community service projects during regular school hours in the spring. This program is written into a staff person's responsibilities, and each student is responsible for documenting their work, and having the supervising adult submit the required paperwork. No teacher wants to lose more class time, but in my experience, some of the most authentic learning experiences I've seen are during service week when kids leave us for a week, are given responsibility outside our gaze, and have to figure it out. If that's the whole point of education, we need to make that happen, even if it's inconvenient to the normal rhythm of our work lives.

ACTION STEPS

1. **Bring a big problem to the table.** Big, hairy, audacious. Those are the problems that kids need to be wrestling with throughout the year. No matter if they are five or fifteen, kids need an opportunity to be incredible in their service to the community and beyond. Students need to know that their work has an opportunity to connect with similar work around the world.
2. **Make a moment of service an ethic of service.** Moving service in the community from an event to a part of life in a classroom is the same shift as having projects at the end of a unit and truly becoming a project-based learning classroom. The shift can be subtle, but the impact can be incredibly large for those being supported.
3. **Document the service of students.** It is important to document previous work completed by kids in the community. Students can get nervous about being in the community and interacting with individuals outside their comfort zone. Having pictures, videos, and written descriptions of the work allows some of these early nerves to be replaced with a leaning into the service.
4. *****Be humble.** This seems like a strange action step for educators, but demonstrating humility with students begins to model an orientation necessary to serve well. It is rarely developmentally dominate for humility to be at the core of the thinking of students in our classrooms. Model humility, and allow conversations about the power of humility in service emerge in the classroom.

RESOURCES

Bringing kids closer to the realities of people, pocketbook, and planet lies at the heart of the connected classroom, and it is married to learning found in the curriculum and standards of Education for Sustainability. When these are explored in the classroom, students find fresh motivation for learning. It is in these learning moments that innovative ideas and solutions emerge that can be brought back to the community for scaling.

When Helping Hurts: How to Alleviate Poverty Without Hurting the Poor . . . and Yourself (http://www.amazon.com/When-Helping-Hurts-Alleviate-Yourself/dp/0802457061)

Americorps and the Corporation for National and Community Service (http://www.nationalservice.gov/programs/americorps)

Emily Pilloton TED Talk on Design, Service, Community Change (http://www.ted.com/talks/emily_pilloton_teaching_design_for_change)

CHAPTER 16

Connecting the Pieces

This chapter begins to bring together the ideas of the book, painting the picture of how connected learners, both adults and kids, have the power to transform learning.

ESSENTIAL QUESTIONS

1. How many different aspects of the connected classrooms can courageous teachers take on at once?
2. What does building a different classroom instead of a better classroom look like?
3. Why do leaders struggle to equip the best teachers with what they need?

THE THEORY

Connecting kids to their learning is of paramount importance to the work of building excellence in schools, but being this artist of learning takes courage. It takes someone who is willing to push back against the system, take positive risks for kids, and be willing to rise above the perpetual tug toward the median. This work can be exhausting. It can be draining both professionally and personally, but it doesn't have to be. Like-minded educators from around the globe are embracing leading connected classrooms, and they are leaning on the wisdom of one another to build the most fulfilling of careers. They are finding new energy in this work, and a fulfillment of their desire to serve kids.

When seeing these courageous teachers in action, the first obvious distinction is that students are in the center of the learning. Their desires, their passions, their wisdom are all front and center in the classroom. Students take control of their learning. The sameness of the learning is vastly overshadowed by the individual paths for growth that are being carved in the classroom sand on a daily basis. The connected classroom uses the simple, yet never mastered, concepts of choice, voice, and authentic audience to create engaging learning opportunities for kids. Choice comes in a variety of flavors including what students learn, how they learn it, and in what ways they showcase their learning, as seen in Figure 4. Voice in the connected classroom includes having students in a continuous dialogue about the norms and culture of the classroom as well as empowering their voice to transcend the walls of the classroom, so they understand the promise of their ideas as citizens. Authentic audience allows all students to realize that school learning is life learning and that the work taking place in school is valued by the adults and experts beyond the walls of the school. Authentic audience provides context while raising the quality of work naturally without the gimmicks of external motivation to make kids work harder.

FIGURE 4

Three Ways to Promote Student Choice in the Connected Classroom

↓

What to Learn

↓

How to Learn It

↓

How to Showcase the Learning

It is with this set of ingredients that learning can feel alive and purposeful. It is with these elements that learning goes from being done to kids to being done by kids, and it is with these bedrock concepts of connected learning that the best parts of education can resurface for all to grab and begin to use. The connected student, the connected teacher, and the connected classroom are building in strength, but it takes the courage of leaders, teacher leaders, and those who support those in schools to remain focused on building momentum for supporting kids in the learning that will grow them as citizen solutionists.

THE CLASSROOM CONNECTION

Steve J. Moore, a teacher of students in the Kansas City area, tells of the joy of learning that came from his work with giving his students choice, voice, and authentic audience. Steve reminds us that the little moments and the smallest actions in teaching can have the biggest impact. He knows artificial chunks of learning that ask all to learn with the same frequency and intensity aren't healthy for kids, students, or communities. He brings hope that a breakthrough for each of us can be right around the corner.

Triangulation is a term many researchers, mathematicians, and scientists are familiar with. It involves the use of multiple sources of information that converge into a point they make together. As an English teacher, triangulation is something I am familiar with in my practice. I consider the impact of a student's efforts and participation during reading and discussion, the generation of writing and visible thinking during a project, and a final product, portfolio, or representation of their learning. These elements together represent a composite whole rather than disconnected series of data. As in geometry, I use the angles I see in student work to determine the point they've reached in their understanding.

In this century of high-speed learning, my use of triangulation almost seems too simple as people learn and explore new ideas faster and through more ubiquitous channels than ever before. We have too many data sources to triangulate, and thus, we need a new technique for making meaning. Teachers and learners need to reshape their conception of how we reach understanding, formulate questions, and establish hunches about important concepts.

As a chemistry student in college, I did many labs where growing crystalline structures was a required task. Unlike simply measuring out of the proper bottles in the right proportions, growing good crystals requires a bit more art and trust in the process. As one would expect, the appropriate ingredients are combined in a beaker first and allowed whatever thermodynamic effects that might come as a result (giving off heat or light, etc.). What's different is that rather than just waiting for the crystals to grow, there needs to be agitation.

Like planting a seedbed, the bottom of the beaker is usually scored a bit with another piece of glass, like a stirring rod, which creates room for seed crystals to take hold.

The agitation is what's interesting. Many reactions require a catalyst, but growing crystals sometimes just doesn't work right until there's a ripple. Just tapping the glass of the beaker ever so slightly can start a wave of crystallization that spreads instantly throughout the solution. It is a truly beautiful process to watch as liquid turns sharply into a more solid form. It's like a fast-motion video of snowflakes accumulating and freezing. The process doesn't end with the agitation, much to the contrary. The most beautiful growths begin with the wave and then are built upon over time as the solution develops and is allowed to fully react.

What this illustrates is a complex, nonlinear processes that requires both technical and artful skill to perform. I believe that a connected presence as a student or educator works in much the same way.

I started teaching in a world where Twitter, blogs, and Web 2.0 were buzzwords. During my preservice education, I slowly developed a personal learning network (PLN) that started with a blog of my first year of teaching. My small, but intentional, efforts as a blogger were matched by an equally small audience on Twitter. Through established channels of discussion, such as the #edchat and meaningful searching, I began to generate discussion, dialogue, and debate about issues pertaining to my teaching. These were the ingredients, the vital components of my professional "solution."

After I got a sense of exactly what I had crafted, I began to step back and examine it more closely. My PLN, in the context of my writing and teaching, was like the beaker full of precrystallized solution back on my lab table in college; it just needed some agitation for something unique and beautiful to happen. In the end, this is the key for the connected classroom as well. It is about having the right components, the right agitation, and the ability to step back and allow learning to grow.

ACTION STEPS

1. **Stop getting better.** Seems like advice that no school leader would ever give until it is coupled with the idea of getting different. Different classrooms are the ones that kids remember. They remember the classroom teachers who had the courage to try something different, no matter whether it failed or succeeded. Choose different today.
2. **Embrace teaching and learning as lifestyle.** Becoming a connected leader of learning is exhausting. It means different hours and different priorities. The early stages of being connected require a huge amount time and energy, but the payoff comes when the loneliness of running a connected classroom fades into a huge pillow of support from those around the globe working just as hard for kids.
3. ***__Move the paint.__** This is a basketball reference to the place where the big players usually spend the majority of their time. If you as a teacher have a place in your classroom where spend significant amounts of time talking or sitting, then move your paint. The rooms were the best learning takes place rarely have places where the teacher is the center of things.
4. ***__Solve an issue.__** There is a need for teachers to vent. The work is brutally hard. This doesn't mean that there shouldn't be time to repair and fix the systems in the school. No one has to be a victim of the system. Teacher voice can solve problems in their system, and it provides students with an example of how their teachers match their words to their actions.

RESOURCES

Connected learning brings together the loneliest innovative classrooms on the planet. As classrooms connect beyond their walls, a new level of support emerges. It is a level of support that lifts spirits and pushes learning experiences forward. These links point to authors who have brought these concepts to the forefront in the form of books and templates for teachers to use to accelerate this process.

> The Courage to Teach—Exploring the Inner Landscape of a Teacher's Life (http://www.amazon.com/The-Courage-Teach-Exploring-Landscape/dp/0470580704)

Personal Learning Networks—Using the Power of Connections to Transform Education (http://www.amazon.com/Personal-Learning-Networks-Connections-Transform/dp/193554327X)

Harvard Project Zero—Visible Thinking (http://www.visiblethinkingpz.org/VisibleThinking_html_files/VisibleThinking1.html)

CHAPTER 17

Educational Leaders as the Catalysts of Change

The urgency to act has always been a struggle for the best educators. Schools looking to avoid being left behind need to accelerate the pace of growth and change in their learning spaces.

ESSENTIAL QUESTIONS

1. Where are the places in your organization where braking is keeping progress from happening?
2. How do we convince a larger audience that both short-term and long-term changes are a part of the overall solution in building educational excellence?
3. How have you placed the armor of being a connected leader on your shoulders?

THE THEORY

After years of watching the top cyclists turn themselves inside out for three weeks each year in the grand tours, one truism has jumped across into change making in education. It is the concept that each touch of the brakes lessens your chance for success. Education has an excess of braking. There is braking for committee meetings. There is braking to find out if there are rules and regulations for or against the innovation at hand. There is braking because of the fear of being seen as a rebel or a lone wolf. There is braking to look around to see if someone else will take up the tempo. All of this braking creates leaders just waiting for a chance to wait again.

Breaking this cycle of braking requires an open and transparent conversation about transforming how learning needs to exist in a more complex and rapidly changing world. Too often, the conversation about education drifts to testing, standards, and teacher evaluation. These are all essential conversations, but these are braking conversations. They brake momentum. They brake the spirit of the innovative, and they brake the road to excellence.

In an open dialogue, one of the first things on the table is the complexity of teaching and learning. This complexity has grown at a tremendous rate, and it has created the need for teachers to be proficient in so many different areas of making learning excellent. We have to acknowledge this shift. We have to celebrate the hard work of those folks growing as teacher leaders, and we have to think about the need to retain, motivate, and grow the excellence that exists in many of our classrooms.

With this at the core of the conversation, the shifts needed for excellence to emerge in more spaces can begin. In our transparent and open conversation, we need to be realistic about how long it takes systematic change to take hold. Big, sustainable change takes five to seven years to be realized. This doesn't mean that impactful, real change for kids can't be a part of those years, but it is essential that long-term work for the ecosystem isn't swept up by the tides of fads or quick fixes. It takes real leadership including both the classroom leader and the district leader to communicate persistently about the road forward.

Education is struggling to scale and build the leaders who want this role and/or have the courage to make this a part of their mission. While this remains a reality, it is imperative that groups of people and networks begin to rally, without braking, to forge an alliance for innovative learning. Organic groups should be coming together with intensity for best practices—practices known to engage and empower learners. Whether it is through providing students choice in how they showcase their work; magnifying the beautiful voices inside students; providing students with a real-world, authentic audience; or using the classroom as a place to literally change the world, classroom leaders have more power than ever to join together with pockets of excellence around the planet. The system of education designed to lift the next generation to be robust citizens is breaking. The road forward is through the daily dedication of the connected classrooms throughout the country. The beauty of learning that comes from these courageous teachers can reshape how education survives.

THE CLASSROOM CONNECTION

Krissy Venosdale is currently an innovation coordinator working with an inspiring staff and eager learners in Houston, Texas. Prior to this role, she inspired young learners and adults in Missouri through her energy and ideas. She believes in the power of connecting with other educators around the world to bring authentic learning experiences together for amplification of understanding through shared goals. By opening classroom doors to the world, she hopes that students and teachers will both see that learning goes far beyond the books and the pages of a curriculum. Learning is about the world and what we can do to make it better.

Used with permission from Krissy Venosdale.

I'm a teacher who dreams. I dream of ways to connect my kids both inside and beyond the classroom. I'm getting closer to bringing one of these dreams to life. It is amazing to think about the possibility. Read along and dream with me.

I want kids to experience learning 24 hours a day for nine months that brings such deep joy and emotion to the table that they will always thirst for knowledge, ideas, and a better world. My idea hatched in a classroom, long before I was a teacher, when I would daydream about creative adventures and wish for bigger learning experiences than the pile of pages put before me. I can remember being a kid, wishing school would be more than it was. I was constantly hungry for bigger learning. I wanted a flame where there was a tiny flicker.

Years later, I became a teacher, and that hunger remains. I look into the eyes of students who lose hope as they grow older, who need something different. Kids looking for learning that will satisfy their powerful hunger to know, to connect, and to understand the world around them. School needed to be more back then, and they still need to be more now.

What if I could change that? What if joy returned? What if there was a school where kids traveled for nine months to experience the beauty of the country? They would write like Lewis and Clark. They would photograph like Ansel Adams. They would paint like Georgia O'Keefe. They would question everything around them, never because it was an assignment but because their passion wouldn't allow them to stop. What if I could change it all and rescue that girl who was starving at her desk, wishing for more, and in turn rescue the kids I see in front of me?

Since then, I've fleshed out what this school would look like for kids. I'd begin with a trip to the east. I'd load 16 students and another teacher into two large vans. We would be gone from September 1 through October 15 learning at primary locations surrounding history and science. We would cover Pennsylvania, New York, New England, and New York City. Washington, DC would be the final piece of this journey. Students would blog and share. They would e-mail and connect. They would be seeking to discover authentic issues about which they could feel their passion for learning grow. I get excited just thinking about it.

I'd imagine that parents would love the idea, but struggle to envision it, as it would be so different from their experience in school. I also wonder about the courage of parents to allow their students to participate. I know that this learning would be the type of disruptive learning that would transform a community. I know that students who learned this way would never allow their kids to learn the way that most schools demanded. I have other legs of the trip designed in my head as well. I continue to dream about learning with kids on a journey, teaching with the sunset staring me in the eyes, and having the soil and dirt that is foundational to this country between my fingers. I dream of taking kids to experience history, breathing in the air of life and exhaling understanding. This would be my connected dream, a dream from which I'd hope to never awake.

ACTION STEPS

1. **Be the cheerleader for change.** Kids need change makers. They need vocal, persistent, dedicated change makers. Change is about timing, politics, resources, and persuasion. It is complex and difficult, but it needs courageous connected educators. Look at the children in front of you and ask yourself whether it is OK to wait another year.
2. **Make your change someone else's change.** Not every change is right for every school, but this doesn't mean that you can't export your best stuff. Sharing isn't bragging. Sharing is our duty. Allow one of your best ideas to be adopted by another classroom and support it through implementation.
3. **Have dreams bigger than today's realities.** If you could start your own school today and implement all your ideas, then you need some bigger ideas. It is wonderful to believe and hold in your heart incredible best practices for kids, but it will be the connected and courageous who can think beyond tomorrow who serve our mission field the greatest.
4. *****Close the experience gap.** It is in experiences that we find beauty, passion, and the drive to change big things. It is in experiences that we mold memories and exercise our smiles. It is in experiences that true, deep, connected learning takes place. Allow your focus to remain on building a classroom that experiences life, liberty, and the pursuit of happiness.

RESOURCES

Expanding change beyond its point of origin has never been a strong point for education, but it is possible to scale change in the connected classroom with the support of building- and district-level leadership and a strong professional learning network. The thoughts of the authors in the resources coupled with the opportunity of expeditionary learning seem like a great starting place for teachers really dedicated to being the change that they envision.

Bob Sutton and Huggy Rao, *Scaling Up Excellence: Getting to More Without Settling for Less* (http://crownpublishing.com/news/scaling-up-excellence-with-robert-i-sutton-and-huggy-rao/#.U92h70BdUds)

Office Hours Podcast (http://www.danpink.com/office-hours/bob-sutton-and-huggy-rao/)

Expeditionary Learning (http://elschools.org/)

Ron Berger—*An Ethic of Excellence* (http://www.heinemann.com/products/E00596.aspx)

Index